THE WILDCATTER

Also by Kenneth Harris

TRAVELLING TONGUES: DEBATING ACROSS AMERICA
KENNETH HARRIS TALKING TO
CONVERSATIONS
ABOUT BRITAIN
ATTLEE

THE
WILDCATTER

A Portrait of Robert O. Anderson

by KENNETH HARRIS

Weidenfeld & Nicolson
NEW YORK

For Barbara,

without whom this book would not have been written

Grateful acknowledgment is made to the University of Oklahoma Press for permission to reprint two excerpts from: *From the Rio Grande to the Arctic: The Story of the Richfield Oil Corporation* by Charles S. Jones, Foreword by Robert O. Anderson. Copyright © 1972 by the University of Oklahoma Press.

Published by Weidenfeld & Nicolson, New York
A Division of Wheatland Corporation
10 East 53rd Street
New York, NY 10022

Published in Canada by General Publishing Company, Ltd.

Library of Congress Cataloging-in-Publication Data
Harris, Kenneth, 1919–
    The wildcatter: a portrait of Robert O. Anderson.

    Includes index.
    1. Anderson, Robert O., 1917–   . 2. Businessmen—
United States—Biography.   3. Petroleum industry and
trade—United States—History.   4. Atlantic Richfield Co.
—History. I. Title.
HD9570.A53H37   1987   338.7′622338′0924   [B]   87-8183
ISBN 1-55584-048-5

Manufactured in the United States of America
Designed by Irving Perkins Associates
First Edition
10 9 8 7 6 5 4 3 2 1

INTRODUCTION

Not long after I got to know Bob Anderson, the founder and former chief executive officer of ARCO, it occurred to me that somebody, possibly Bob himself, ought to make a record of his life and his career. Both were colorful and varied, and as full of contrast as his elegant Savile Row suits with his Stetson hat.

There was certainly material for a story: Bob had begun in the oil industry with a one-third share in a small refinery employing a dozen or so men, and by a series of purchases and mergers had built up what became the seventh largest oil company in the United States, with himself as chairman, chief executive and major shareholder. Beginning with no land at all, he had become the largest individual rancher in the United States, and now owns nearly a million acres in Texas, New Mexico and Wyoming. He had twice been asked to fill an unexpired term in the United States Senate, twice been asked to serve as American ambassador to Great Britain, and once been offered the position of secretary of the Treasury. He had at one time or another held every nonelective office in the national Republican Party. A personal friend of three American Presidents, his advice had frequently been solicited by other residents of the White House. Under his chairmanship, and with his financial backing, the Aspen Institute had been transformed from an inward-looking academic institution into an international authority on world affairs. He was a patron of the theater, music and the opera. A museum was shortly to be built and named for him. He was a famous breeder of cattle and horses, an avid sportsman and a pioneer environmentalist. His acquisition of a great British newspaper had preserved its character and editorial independence. For these and other reasons it seemed desirable that his life and activities be recorded.

There was only one obstacle: Bob Anderson himself. For a long time he was interested neither in writing his biography nor in having it written. Over the years he has given some—not many—interviews to newspapers or television stations and has made numerous speeches. But though Bob is an easy person to work with, he is not easy to get on paper. People meeting him at public occasions or at private parties find him a relaxed and friendly extrovert, but, as they would discover on better acquaintance, he is in fact fundamentally uncommunicative, at heart a loner. "The more you see of Bob," one of his friends has said, "the less you get to know him."

It was hardly to be expected that such a man would greet the idea of a book about himself with enthusiasm. Whatever desire Bob had to communicate was in any case assuaged by his many public activities. On top of this, he felt that he had far too many things to do to talk to a would-be biographer. Rather than try—and with what success?—to remember past glories or answer a biographer's questions, Bob would want to be doing things: another business deal; a newly drilled well to inspect; a visit to the Aspen Institute; a speech to a gathering of environmentalists; some new cattle to be looked at; the purchase of nine local banks to be negotiated; the eighteenth grandchild to be christened. And if there *were* some spare time, there was duck to be hunted, trout to be caught and a ride into the hills with his wife, Barbara. Far, far too much to do.

A biographer might have hoped to surmount these obstacles by a judicious use of Anderson's diaries and letters. Such a hope would have been short-lived. Bob did keep a diary, but only from ages twelve to eighteen, a sparse and laconic one at that, the magnitude of the entries diminishing as the number of his years increased. He seems to have begun another diary in 1973, but that, too, soon trickled out. Bob is no Samuel Pepys.

As for his letters, they are practically nonexistent. Aside from his family and his two secretaries he has, according to Barbara, probably written more to me in the last ten years than to anyone. In fact, I have never actually received a letter from him; the half-dozen communications which have come my way are letters written *to* him by others, on top of which he has jotted a few words in his own hand.

There came a day, however, when Bob changed his mind about the book, and this "portrait"—rather than a proper biography—is the result. My participation in it came about as follows:

In November 1976 the British newspaper *The Observer,* for which I worked, was experiencing financial difficulties. Like its owners and some of my colleagues, I was looking for a buyer who was both wealthy enough to support the paper and sufficiently public-spirited to preserve its editorial independence. I mentioned this to several acquaintances, among them a close American friend of twenty-five years' standing, Douglass Cater, now president of Washington College, in Chestertown, Maryland, then an authority on the American—and to some extent British—media. Douglass was on friendly terms with many figures in American public life. He asked me for a full account of *The Observer*'s situation. At the end of it, he simply said, "Perhaps Bob Anderson would be interested." He then went to the telephone. Five days later Bob Anderson owned *The Observer.*

When Bob Anderson arrived in London two weeks later to inspect his new acquisition, I was introduced to him by Douglass not so much as an intermediary in the transaction but as an old friend. Had it not been for my relationship with Douglass, for which I shall always be grateful, I would never have gotten to be a friend of Bob's. It goes without saying that had I not become a friend of Bob's, I would never have been in a position to write *The Wildcatter.*

Work for *The Observer,* the BBC and ARCO took me across the Atlantic sometimes four or five times a year, and consequently I made several visits to Bob's ranch home, the Circle Diamond, near the village of Picacho, New Mexico. Over the years I got to know the

viii   :   *Kenneth Harris*

family: his seven children and eighteen grandchildren; his father, whose ninetieth birthday celebration I attended; his two brothers, his sister and many in-laws. The Andersons are an affectionate and tightly knit group.

A few days before Christmas 1981 I was sitting in the kitchen of the Circle Diamond ranch having breakfast with Bob and Barbara, three of the children and five of the grandchildren. The grandchildren were asking Bob about China, since shortly after Christmas he was to fly to Beijing to sign a historic deal which would allow ARCO to drill there for offshore oil. The grandchildren wanted to know what China and the Chinese were like. Barbara said, as she often had before, "Bob, you really ought to get this down on paper. And lots of other things also, if only for your family." I expressed agreement and offered to serve as an amanuensis; I had spent quite a lot of time with Bob on both sides of the Atlantic. And after all, there was no hurry. "Too many other things to do," said Bob, "and I wouldn't let Kenneth waste his time writing a book about *me.*"

But his mind is never closed, and if he decides to change it he can turn 180 degrees in as many seconds. That same day there came a telephone call from Los Angeles: the Chinese government had postponed the signing of the agreement because of some new problems, which would take time to iron out. This meant that five days which Bob had scheduled for the China trip were suddenly free. He came back into the kitchen and said, "Barbara, let's fly to Alaska." And then he added, "If you have your tape recorder with you, Kenneth, maybe we could make a start on the book."

We taped a couple of hours on the jet to Alaska, and a few more in the hotel room in Anchorage, on New Year's Day, with Barbara present and reminiscing. Over the next few years I recorded Bob between business hours in many places around the world. Most of the interviewing was done in the library at the Circle Diamond, in between playing soccer with the grandchildren, visiting historic sights, walking, riding, fishing and hunting duck.

To me the Circle Diamond ranch seemed a very appropriate setting for the operation. It is his beloved and very private home, and on the average he spends three out of four weekends there. It is the setting and ambience in which his personality most reveals itself. First, he is a family man, and this is the place the family as a whole knows best. Secondly, he has always been a country man. When he was a boy in Chicago his parents took him, his brothers and sister into the country around the city every Sunday, and he came to manhood with a love for nature and the great outdoors. Thirdly, Bob loves ranching and has had many successes in it.

His greatest has been the establishment of the breed of cattle called the Brangus. Thirty-five years ago the best beef steer was considered to be the Hereford. Bob had built up a splendid herd, but the hot sun of the Southwest, he found, made the white skin areas of the Hereford prone to skin cancer. The cows sometimes contracted acute sunburn on their udders, and, the teat being especially sensitive, the mother would kick off the feeding calves. Bob experimented with other breeds and with crossbreeding. Eventually he heard of the South West Research Foundation in San Antonio, Texas, which was experimenting with a cross between Aberdeen Angus and Brahmas. The black skin of this animal was not susceptible to solar pigmentation changes; it would range farther through rough ground for its fodder than most other animals and eat less when it found it. The Brangus drank less water. Nevertheless, the animal carried plenty of flesh, and the meat was lean and tasty. Bob tried the animal, was impressed, made the SWR an offer and acquired their foundation herd. The Brangus today is probably the most rapidly growing breed in the United States.

Another success came from an accidental perception. One day Bob saw a patch of plants growing outside the walls of his hacienda near Durango, Mexico. "They were like pampas grass, with a heavy head of grain on the stalk. I asked what it was: it was triticale, a hybrid, half-rye, half-wheat, containing more protein than either, very hardy, and it could stand drought." He brought an armload of triticale back to the Circle Diamond and began experiments with it. Four years later ARCO began producing triticale on a commercial scale, and though the plant is nowadays being produced in other countries, including Britain, ARCO's seventeen different varieties make it the number-one producer in the world.

Seeing Bob trotting around the ranch on his Arabian stallion or driving around in a jeep, battered Stetson on his head, wearing old blue jeans, a sheepskin jacket and western boots, it is easy to see that the mesquite, not the oil rig, is his spiritual home. Influenced by his father's tales of visits to oil fields where the oil tycoons were also cattlemen, Bob grew up to see a kinship between oil production and ranching. The life of the land appeals not only to the nature lover and environmentalist in him, but also to the historian and romantic.

Although most of the talk for the preparation of this book happened around the ranch, we also conversed in many other places, including Brighton, Britain's most famous seaside resort; Oxford, after seeing what ARCO had done for new shelves in the seventeenth-century Bodleian Library—the greatest book collection in Europe; Stockholm, after a concert in the Royal Palace given for Bob by the king; Berlin, after an East-West relations conference; Paris, after an Aspen conference; Siena, while Bob and Barbara were waiting to see the oldest horse race in the world, the Palio, run bareback round the city square; outside the Forbidden City in Beijing, while he was waiting to sign a treaty with China; and on the way back to London after a day at Royal Ascot, both of us wearing gray top hat and tails.

As well as talking to Bob I have talked to many of his colleagues at Atlantic Richfield and Aspen, to friends who have had no business dealings with him and to people who have come into contact with him for a variety of reasons, either in Europe or the United States.

The following, then, is an account written by one friend about another to set down some information about him while there is time and opportunity to obtain it, and while recollections—those of Bob and of other people—are still significant and fresh. Criticism, reappraisal, perspective and further food for thought can come at a later date.

—K.H.
London, February 1987

THE WILDCATTER

CHAPTER ONE

In 1673, Chicago, recorded by the French explorers Marquette and Joliet as the "Chicago Portage" on Lake Michigan, had been a mere landmark on the route from the Mississippi to the Chicago rivers, and for several decades it remained no more than a trading post. It took its name from the stream which the Indians called Chekagou. The word means "big" or "strong" or "powerful," but the slow river was none of these, and the stream may have gotten its name from the powerful smell of the wild garlic that grew thickly on its banks. In early 1833 the population was under two hundred, but by the end of the year hundreds of people had poured into Chicago to take advantage of the virgin Illinois soil, most of them farmers from New England or unemployed workers from factories in New York. Each year from then on, more and more people, from the East Coast of America and immigrants from Western Europe, headed for Chicago.

By the end of the century, with a population of well over a million, Chicago was the second city of the United States, a city of culture as well as of wealth, its buildings endowed with gardens and parks, stretching for more than twenty miles along the shore of the lake. Eighty percent of the population were immigrants or the children of immigrants. Chicago included the largest Polish, Lithuanian, German and Greek settlements in the United States, but the most numerous of its ethnic groups were the Dutch and Swedes. In 1889 an eighteen-month-old boy who had been brought to America from Helsinborg, Sweden, settled there with his family: Hugo Anderson, Robert Anderson's father.

Hugo's own father, Carl August Anderson, had been born in Husby, Sweden. Orphaned at the age of ten and brought up by his sister, he was later apprenticed at the local Stevens Foundry and became a master pattern maker. Soon after he married Augusta Mardh and moved to Helsinborg.

He was a gentle, easygoing man, whereas Augusta was dynamic and better educated. She was the disciplinarian of the family, and ambitious for her children. Carl's twin sister had emigrated to Chicago. Four years after his marriage, he joined her, got a job and six months later sent for his family. The weather in November was stormy; the voyage was rough. Working largely with sails, the ship took a month to make New York. The mother was ill for nearly the whole voyage.

As a boy, Hugo was intelligent and industrious. He was an avid reader, often up before dawn to read in the kitchen until his mother discovered this practice and put an end to it for his health's sake. At the age of ten, he had a newspaper route. Aged twelve, he taught English to the local jeweler's immigrant brother. He peddled yeast foam, painted fences and tidied up neighboring backyards. He would work from dawn to dusk to earn a few cents of his own. But physically he was very small. When he left school at fourteen to help support the family—his teachers were disappointed that he was not going on with school and college—he looked two or three years younger than his age and was able to ride on streetcars at the reduced fare for children under twelve. He applied for a job in the Marshall Field store and was turned down because, his interviewer said, he could not be more than ten and should go back to school. A family friend in the Evangelical Covenant Church, where the Andersons worshiped, worked in the First National Bank of Chicago. Knowing the boy's character and the family's need for money, he got Hugo a start as a bellboy at the bank.

From his earliest days at the bank, the boy's personality, energy and devotion were noticed by all around him. Everybody saw the pride he took in all his work. He was doing well and earning a good reputation when, in his sixteenth year, he did something which deeply impressed his bosses. At the time he was running errands for August Blum, then assistant to the bank's president, James B. Forgan. One morning, when the boy was in the room, Forgan asked Blum for a recent report on the affairs of a bank in St. Louis. A deal of some magnitude depended on Forgan's obtaining the information immediately. Blum did not know where to look for it and was worried. When he and young Hugo were alone, the boy spoke up: "There's an out-of-town newsstand across the street. The report could be in a St. Louis newspaper." He ran across the street. "It seems a miracle today," he recorded sixty years later, "but I rummaged through the newspapers and found the one I wanted." Blum was delighted and took him and the newspaper to Forgan's office. "What we couldn't think of, this boy did," he told the president.

From that day on, Hugo made his way up in the bank with steadiness and speed, becoming clerk, assistant cashier, cashier, assistant loans officer, loans officer, vice president and eventually first executive vice president. He retired at seventy after fifty-six years of service. Long before that he had become one of the best-known bankers in America. He acquired a reputation for integrity, outspokenness and moral courage. On more than one occasion, he rose from behind his desk, buttoned his jacket across an extended chest—though short, he was robustly built—and threatened his visitor with assault if a remark was not withdrawn. He was also known for his sanguine view of human nature and general faith in life—symbolized by the jaunty angle at which he always wore his banker's homburg.

His achievements in his professional life did not prevent him from undertaking a variety of civic responsibilities. When he was sixteen, a professor at the University of Chicago who had met him through his church activities took him to meet the president of the university, William Rainey Harper. "Hugo," said Dr. Harper, "I have heard a good deal about you from our mutual friend here and would like to bring you to the university to finish your education. You write shorthand; we can give you employment to take care of your expenses." Hugo declined, but the offer moved him greatly, and he made up his mind to do voluntary work for every institution which had helped him in his development. Consequently, he taught in Sunday school, founded a boys' club and a Bible class, was on the committee of the church's Young People's Society and played the leading role in setting up the Chicago YMCA Liberal Arts College, founded to give an education to students who had failed to qualify for entrance to a university. For many years he was president of the board of trustees of North Park College and Theological Seminary, and president of the Fourth Presbyterian Church. Only in one respect did he not win the approbation of his fellow Swedes in Chicago: because he was so proud to be an American he would not go out of his way to preserve the church's use of the Swedish language. He felt it might become a barrier to assimilation. This attitude did not prevent him from later having a Chair for Swedish Studies established in his name at North Park College. Before he died peacefully in his ninety-seventh year, he had been awarded honors by three Swedish kings.

Hilda Nelson, Bob Anderson's mother, was born in Chicago. She was a beautiful and able girl, interested in music and books. When her father died, comparatively young, she decided that for the next three years she would give her earnings to her mother. Hugo first saw her singing in the choir, and it was love at first sight. After they became engaged, she kept her well-paid job as secretary to the president of the Chicago Junction Railroad so that Hugo could do three more years at night school before they married, in 1914. They had four children: Hugo Jr. (born June 11, 1915), Robert (April 13, 1917), Donald (April 6, 1919), and Helen (January 7, 1921)—in her father's words, "the jewel of my family."

The four children grew up in an atmosphere of love, morality and, in the early years, the Christian religion. Hugo, according to Hugo Jr., was "stern, but that doesn't mean he wasn't loving. If there was any conflict between the two, the love won out." He was a strong father, but he wasn't a critical father. "In fact, if he had a fault it was that he wasn't tough enough with us." He did not impose his sense of right and wrong upon them, but hoped they would grow to share it. "You might think that a father who had come up through life as he had, making it all on his own, would try to instill in his sons a desire to succeed. Not at all. He used to say, 'I don't care what you do in life so long as it's honest.' It didn't have to be important. The main thing was to have peace of mind in what you were doing."

Though Hugo and Hilda had plenty of friends and neighbors, they spent much more time than most parents with their children. They both enjoyed the outdoor life. There were many places to visit by car or train not far from Chicago, and when Hugo could afford a car, the family would spend the weekend in the open air, walking, picnicking, fishing and, when the weather was right, swimming. The children took this love of nature for granted, grew up with and in it. "My mother and father knew every flower and tree they saw," said Bob's elder brother, Hugo. "They knew nothing about birds, but my mother gave me a book about them, and Bob and I became amateur ornithologists."

In the 1930s, when the three boys were in their teens, the Andersons were living an upper-middle-class life in a large ten-room ground-floor apartment—five bedrooms, living room, dining room, kitchen, quarters for one maid, sunporch, small backyard and small front yard—at 57th and Dorchester Avenue, a few blocks from the university. It was rented because Hugo did not believe in buying real estate. Hugo, now a vice president, rose steadily in the hierarchy of the bank, and had acquired some capital and a Packard car—not so much as he might have had, since he refused on principle to invest in any enterprise to which he was advising the bank to lend money. Notwithstanding, he was doing well, his family enjoying all—and more than—he had been brought up to consider desirable. Then in 1932 came a severe setback. Early that year, Franklin Delano Roosevelt ordered all banks closed. Banks in Chicago failed right and left. Hugo lost most of his substantial capital. Fortunately for the family, he and his wife had always lived well within their income, never on credit, and very simply. (Only Hugo Jr. caught a glimpse of some deprivation: one day his father sat down opposite him, and Hugo Jr. saw a hole in the sole of his father's shoe. The father always dressed well. When his son asked him why there was a hole in his shoe, the father answered evasively. When a few years later Hugo had once again made himself comfortably rich, the boys did not notice any change in their standard of living except for a second car.)

Hugo Anderson regretted that he had left school at fourteen and resolved that his children should have the best education available. With this in mind, he had rented the family apartment within a few blocks of the University of Chicago, and of the University High School and Elementary School. Hugo had heard much about these schools in his early years at the bank, and he had kept up his friendship with William Rainey Harper, who at one stage asked him to leave the bank and take an administrative job at the university. The University Elementary School and the University High School were experimental—both were "laboratory schools," as their founder, Professor John Dewey, had described them—conducted with the participation of professors at the university so that a new curriculum linking all three stages of education into a continuous unit could be developed and made available to the high schools of the whole country through the publication of specially produced textbooks. Important parts of the experiment were the change in the university's year from three to four terms or quarters, the fourth quarter to be a kind of summer school for people already out at work; the organization of extension lectures; the elimination of the eighth grade at the elementary school and the transfer of its seventh grade to the high school; and the fusion of the last two years of the high school with the first two years of the college. The combination of the educational experimentation and the fact that about three quarters of the pupils of the high school were the children of the university's faculty members meant that its academic standards were unusually high. The location of the Anderson home meant that Bob and his siblings were reared in an academic atmosphere.

As a schoolboy Bob was very outgoing. "He got on easily with people," his brother Hugo recalls. "For instance, if we went on a trip and wanted to ask for directions, and Bob went into the local store to ask for them, Donald or I would have to go in after fifteen minutes and drag him out. He'd get involved in conversation, ask about what was going on in the town, the weather—just about anything. If Donald or I had gone in to get the information, we'd have been out in a couple of minutes." Donald, too, thought of him, at that stage, as an extrovert. "He was always something of a leader; his friends were quite strong characters, but he seemed to lead them; they would congregate at *our* house. It wasn't that he was assertive, but that they were attracted to him. He was creative, had ideas; they found him interesting; they'd follow him. Even in high school I thought he would outperform the rest of his friends." But there was another side to Bob. "He was maddeningly absentminded," said his sister, Helen. She complained that when she walked down the street with him he would often look through his friends as if they weren't there. All agreed that he could at times be annoyingly detached, and that sometimes when he should have been around, he was missing. Helen remembers her mother once getting angry with him. Their father was away for some days, so the mother took all four away for the weekend in the family car. At the end of the weekend, while they were loading the car to go home, Mrs. Anderson saw that Bob was standing by, doing nothing, "dreaming." She said sharply, "Bob, the car's packed, and you've done nothing to help the whole weekend. Go back up to the rooms and bring down anything that's left." Bob went, and in a few minutes returned, carrying two Gideon Bibles.

At school, Bob did not aspire to write, but now and again when the mood took him, he would "sound off," and some scraps of his never lengthy effusions were preserved to amuse the other members of the family. One page of a diminutive notebook is headed "Pattern for Higher Living—Outstanding English customs that I think should be carried to America." The only two which have survived are:

1. *Tea* (not unknown in the US but should be drunk more frequently. . . .)
2. *Adjourning after meals for coffee* in two separate groups, ladies and gentlemen. Very restful, and breaks the monotony of the evening. Maybe faintly Victorian but should be revived for the sake of better living and entertainment. Might not work here with our pseudo-sophisticated children.

He also wrote an editorial for the school magazine suggesting how he and his fellow students could improve on the benefits they had derived from their education. It began:

After the Battle of Waterloo, Napoleon had plenty of time to think over his errors and figure out just what he would do if he could re-live his life.

> Although I have not met my Waterloo, I cannot help but think of how I would go through school if I was re-entering my junior year. In this informal essay, I am first going to attempt to show how I think the pupils of U-High can get the most of school.

He outlined a work program entitled "From Kindergarten to a degree in fourteen years," the proposal consisting largely of taking extra courses—"rather stiff but it will pay in the long run."

Though Bob had no literary aspirations, he was not averse to putting pen to paper. He kept a diary from the age of twelve intermittently until he went to college, resuming it from time to time in later years, usually by way of notes on trips and holidays. In his boyhood and youth, his notes were mainly about what he saw rather than what he did or thought, though here and there are some reflections, especially about his favorite sport—fishing.

> In his *Proverbs* Solomon tells us that a fine spirit causes a flourishing age, that is an age that is ripe and long. I would say that pleasing amusements and proper sports cause a ripe old age. One of the finest sports is fishing with a rod, line and hook. However, I do not pursue the gentle art of angling because of Solomon's opinion about how to have a flourishing old age, or even because fishing is such a healthy sport, but merely because I have become a semi-maniac about it.

Closest to Bob among his friends was Bob Merriam. The two had gone to kindergarten together, to elementary and high school, and then to college. "He was always a pretty outgoing personality," recalls Merriam, "a *jolly* personality, amusing, cheering, good to be with. He was an easy mixer, but he went his own way when he wanted to. He had natural curiosity—scientific curiosity. He wanted to know how things worked, not that he had a great mechanical bent—just curiosity. He read a great deal, a very great deal—he'd read anything—classics or comics, thrillers—anything."

In his last year of high school, Bob wondered whether to enter the University of Chicago or seek fresh pastures in one of the large Eastern universities like Harvard or one of the smaller colleges like Dartmouth or Williams. His indecision came quickly to an end when in 1935 he was offered a four-year scholarship at the University of Chicago. It was a unique scholarship. Only one was granted every year, and its holder was free to study what he chose for the entire four years without being required to reach any academic level of achievement or to specialize in any particular course of study. It was another expression of the university's commitment to the idea that all students should be given maximum freedom. Attendance at lectures was not compulsory, the emphasis of the curriculum being on self-education. The theme was that broadness of culture, not academic specialization, was the goal for the civilized man.

As it happened, Bob was being borne along on an early wave of experimentation launched by the new chancellor of the university, Dr. Robert Maynard Hutchins, by which pupils in the last year of the University High School could take the first year of the university's Humanities course. This enabled him to indulge his curiosity.

Bob Merriam's father, Charles Merriam, a distinguished professor of history, was a member of President Franklin D. Roosevelt's Brain Trust. Young Merriam was then a New Deal Democrat, interested in international affairs as well as in American politics. "Bob would listen with the greatest good nature to me holding forth," says Bob Merriam, "but it was clear that I was more interested than he was in the social movements of the day." What interested Bob more than talk about the New Deal was what he was hearing about the harnessing of atomic power, the social implications of which fascinated him. From talk with the sons of some of the professors of atomic research then at the University of Chicago, including Arthur Holly Compton and Harvey Bruce Lemon, both later to play a major role in the production of the atomic bomb, he formed an idea of what might be accomplished if the atom were made to provide unlimited and inexpensive energy in the service of humankind, a source of energy with which at several points in his later life he was to be connected.

At this time, Bob Anderson began to think about not one, but two possible careers—an academic career and a business career. The attraction of an academic career was before his eyes and all around him—intelligent, articulate, cultivated people, living the professional life which they found rewarding in itself. This attraction was exemplified for him in the person of John Nef, the internationally famous economic historian who, at the personal invitation of Robert Hutchins, had left Harvard to become professor of economic history at the University of Chicago.

Nef was born in 1899, and after a brilliant career at Harvard, lived for five years in Europe, doing research for his historical works. His magnum opus, *The Rise of the British Coal Industry,* still regarded as a classic, was published in 1932. The following year the Nefs moved into the Dorchester Avenue apartment house where the Andersons lived, occupying the apartment immediately across the hall from them. Hugo Sr. and John Nef got to know each other, and soon brought about a family friendship which has lasted to this day.

As well as a distinguished academic, John Nef was a sophisticated and cultured man, much traveled in Europe, with the wealth to pursue his interests and indulge his tastes. He brought his friends Pablo Picasso, Igor Stravinsky, Arnold Schoenberg, Artur Schnabel, Jacques Maritain and T. S. Eliot to the university and involved Marc Chagall in a teaching program he had devised which fulfilled his ambition to break down specialization and build bridges between the sciences and the arts. "He liked comforts as well as culture," said Bob. "As well as his collection of first editions, his Chagalls and Picassos, he had a magnificent cellar and kept a splendid table. He was not a hairshirt academic."

Every year the Nefs went for several months to Europe, where they were on friendly terms with leading politicians, academics, writers, painters and poets, spending part of the time in European capitals, part in holidaying on the French Riviera. The Nefs, childless but fond of children, knew all four Anderson children well and took a special fancy to Bob. When they were a man short, the Nefs invariably asked Bob to come to dinner. Through the Nefs, he met, as well as leading American writers, musicians and artists, academics from abroad like Professor R. H. Tawney, the voice of the British Labour movement; Sir John Clapham, then the president of the Royal Academy; Arnold Toynbee, the historian; Sir William Beveridge, master of University College, Oxford, later of welfare state fame; and the Labour Party theorist Professor Harold Laski. Nef did more than anyone, with the exception of his father, to interest Bob in the academic world; and Nef's belief in the unity of all knowledge, the union of the arts with the sciences, deeply impressed him.

But Bob had already perceived two things about academic life. The first had come to him one day when he helped Nef on with his raincoat. It looked like any other raincoat, but it was lined with mink. The great majority of academics were impecunious, and being poor were vulnerable to what he saw as the first drawback of an academic vocation: it could be "cabin'd, cribb'd, and confin'd," cut off from, or only imperfectly reflecting, the outside, the *real* world. The second drawback to life on the campus, he concluded, was that those who lived the whole of their life in college were in danger of becoming small-minded. The atmosphere of the university could breed pettiness and jealousy. Some professors lacked perspective. Bob resolved that if he *did* teach at a university, it would be after he had made enough money to enable him to live the kind of academic life that John Nef lived—researching and vacationing abroad, and entertaining his distinguished friends at home.

He had no inclination to teach business. He had already decided that "teaching business in school is like teaching swimming without water." He was interested in geology, partly because he had heard his father talk about it when he reminisced about the oil industry, partly because the subject fascinated him. He took it as an extra subject, and did so well his professor advised him to turn his whole attention to it and qualify to teach it. He was also interested in astronomy. "All natural phenomena interested me." He had an outstanding head for figures and could calculate rapidly in his head, frequently beating his colleagues using slide rules. But mathematics as a subject did not appeal to him. If it came to teaching he would have taught philosophy, particularly classical philosophy. "It was practical—they applied what they thought, or tried to, to the running of society. They philosophized about people, and government, and personal morality, not about the meaning of words." But to be a philosopher, even more than to be some other kind of teacher, required some wealth—the means to get to know the outside world, the world men had to live in, and to be independent: "How can a philosopher living in poverty have a full and balanced view of what the world is all about? And be free to speak the truth about it?" So went his thoughts about the pros and cons of academic life.

But there was a second attraction: the oil industry. In his teens Bob heard much about the oil industry from his father. In the 1930s Hugo Sr. had acquired a unique reputation in the oil and banking worlds: he was the only banker who would make loans to oilmen while their oil was still in the ground—on trust. This was an extremely risky business, and for many years while he was loans officer he met with resistance from his colleagues. His argument was that he knew and could judge the men he lent to, and if they were convinced that the oil was there, then he would back them. Besides, he said, most of these men already banked with the First National on account of their other operations—farming, cattle-raising, construction companies and so on—so that in the event of failure on the loan in oil, their other assets could be realized. Not one of the loans he made ever proved ill advised. He made millions out of oil for the First National Bank. By the end of the thirties he was beyond criticism, and knew more about oil and oilmen than any other American banker.

Hugo did more than make money for oilmen and for the bank. He had a great effect on the world oil industry by enabling the development of a whole new class of oil producers. The difficulty of getting money to fund their high-risk operations meant that the industry was dominated by large-scale corporations cautiously financed by the major banks. Hugo's loans were made to the small independent risk-taker who frequently began with only a drilling rig. Such an operator would come to Hugo, and if he made his case, could borrow enough money to drill a well. If the well made good, he could borrow enough to drill another. There are now about 60,000 independent oil companies in the United States, many of them the second or third generation of Hugo's original clients.

One of the reasons for Hugo's success was his personal knowledge of the many plants and the terrains. To get that knowledge, throughout several years he had made weekend expeditions to see for himself how the borrowers lived and the prospects on which he was being asked to lend. He made frequent trips into Oklahoma and Texas, and on returning home would hold forth at the dinner table to his wife and children, telling them colorful tales of the men and the sights he had seen. He talked well. He was also a keen and talented home movie-maker, and often took his movie camera with him. Bob Anderson listened avidly to these enthusiastic stories and gazed at the arresting films of this risk-laden frontier life. The oilmen frequently came to Chicago to talk with Hugo. While still a boy, Bob met dozens of them, big cigar-smoking, be-Stetsoned John Wayne figures who arrived in their own planes, having flown for hours to have lunch with their banker, and flew back home again to Tulsa or Houston in time for dinner. "They were the Saudi Arabians of the 1930s," he says today. Such men often combined oil operations with ranching. Ranching, too, was rich and colorful. Vast fortunes had been made with a cowboy background. It was a life which brought much of the American frontier era of the not too distant past right back into the present day. The young Bob Anderson was fascinated by all this. It was a life of risk, and his father's example had taught him to take risk in his stride. He had heard that his father's colleagues had often tried to prevent him from taking risks until they realized how much money this successful risk-taking was bringing back to the bank—a lesson Bob learned and never forgot. He saw a connection between the oil and cattle millionaires and John Nef's Chagalls and his mink-lined raincoat. It struck him that in this exciting outdoor existence, so different from that of the bank, he might make enough money to enable him to retire early and live the best kind of academic life. At this time he would occasionally mention to Hugo Jr. or Bob Merriam, in a tone half-jocular, half-serious, that he had decided to become an oil millionaire and retire at forty. But jocular or serious, that was what he had decided to do: make enough money in business to last him the rest of his life, and then, while relatively young, turn his mind to the world of creativity and ideas.

The four years Bob spent at the University of Chicago, from 1935 to 1939, had two great effects upon him. The first was the conclusion that a man's best teacher is himself. "There is practically nothing they can teach you in a university which you can't learn out of books in the public library if you've got the will to learn. Maybe that's the *best* way to learn—if you've got access to somebody who you can go to occasionally if you get bogged down by something you can't understand." Self-teaching and a few tutors. "I was a self-taught astronomer, and I was a self-taught geologist. I once *bet* a guy that in a week I could teach myself enough about the art and science of pottery—not to make pots, you understand, but to *talk* about making pots—to be able to give an hour's lecture on the subject, with slides. I won." His argument was simple. "First of all, in a library you can read a book six times faster than you can hear a guy talk. Secondly, you are not distracted by the theatricality of the lecture room—and maybe by the personality of the lecturer. Thirdly, *you* know what you *want* to know." Though in the forty-five years since he left Chicago he has been involved in academic life and has given a good deal of money to institutions of higher education, he still believes that there should be less money spent on new buildings and facilities and more money spent on encouraging students to learn how to educate themselves.

But the most important thing the University of Chicago did for him was to introduce him to the woman he married: Barbara Phelps. On her father's side, her forebears had come from England to New England in 1630. Her mother's family had also come from England, arriving in Maryland in the 1600s. The men of both families fought in the Revolutionary War. Barbara's father had earned a degree in engineering at Cornell University and then became a successful naval architect. When he was with the Bethlehem Steel Shipyards at Sparrows Point, near Baltimore, he met his wife, Julia Muchette, who had been something of a rebel in her youth. "She left Maryland," recalls Barbara, "marched with the suffragettes, smoked cigarettes in public with Alice Roosevelt Longworth and had a successful career in New York City drawing cartoons for the Sunday *New York Times* and *New York Herald*. She settled down in Baltimore only after she had married." In 1923 the Phelps family moved to Chicago because shipbuilding had come to a standstill after the First World War. Barbara spent her school years in Maryland, and two more years at a finishing school, Gunston Hall, in Washington, D.C. She then moved to the University of Chicago, on her parents' doorstep, where she began to study for a degree in liberal arts with the intention of becoming a writer.

Bob first saw her at the beginning of her first term, sitting near him in the university coffee shop listening to other girls trying to persuade her to join their club. He had not been short of attractive girlfriends, but his first glimpse of Barbara made a great impression on him. He, too, was not shy. He discovered that she was a Chicago girl and that they had mutual friends. He found that as well as having beauty and intelligence, Barbara was as much of an outdoors person as he. He was soon in love. Barbara found him stimulating, good-looking, positive, attentive and purposeful, with a great gift for brightening and amusing people. Above all, he was high-spirited; he could bring a group to life. "A dozen of us would be sitting around and Bob would suddenly appear, and soon we'd all be laughing." Hugo and Hilda found Barbara adorable. The Phelps admired young Bob. Brothers, sisters and parents took to each other. Bob made up his mind that on August 25, 1939, the day of his graduation, he would marry Barbara if she would have him.

She would. She was twenty, he was twenty-two. Bob received his degree at 4 P.M. Two hours later they were married.

CHAPTER TWO

Bob spent the summer vacation of his second year of college working with a pipeline crew at Corpus Christi in the Texas oil fields. His father believed that the boys should have a sight and the feel of what manual labor was about. Hugo Jr. spent a summer on a sheep ranch in Idaho. Donald spent two months working with truck weighers in Chicago. The pipeline was being constructed by the American Mineral Spirits Company of Chicago, clients of Hugo's. On his first day's work, Bob was appointed foreman of the crew because he was the only one who could read and write. The work was hard, the sun hot; the crew was sometimes difficult to handle. But he loved it. There was opportunity to indulge his curiosity. He visited local refineries small enough for an inquisitive youth, with a head for facts and figures and a mechanical sense, to learn about the nuts and bolts. Several wells were being drilled in the vicinity; in the bars and coffee shops he met the small independent wildcatters who were financing them, some on the strength of loans from Hugo Sr.

He got to know his way around a drilling rig, studied the wells already in production and learned the basic processes of the industry. "I was totally absorbed." When Hugo Jr. met him off the plane back in Chicago, he felt that Bob had almost decided to return to Corpus Christi and stay there. "He went on talking about it all the way home, and he went on talking about it when he got there." It was the life that attracted him, and the people he had met, but above all, the opportunities. "Not opportunities for making money. We were too young to be that conscious of money, even then, in the depths of the Depression, when the most menial jobs were hard to get. No, opportunities for initiative, experiment, independence and an outdoor life. I had thought some time before from what Bob had said that he would go into the oil industry, and I knew Dad thought so, too. From now on it was certain."

But oil production was a high-risk operation, requiring high-scale finance. Long before he left the university, Bob had made up his mind that, though he wanted to produce oil, he would have to find some other means to get into the industry. A small refinery was a much less expensive venture and, located in or near the field of production, provided a "listening post" where information about production possibilities could be stored for the day when prospects had reached a point where the risks of drilling were viable. But even if he had had the money to acquire a small refinery he lacked the knowledge to run one. So he went to the company which had employed him in Texas the previous summer and asked for a job. He had made a great impression at Corpus Christi. They knew he would not stay with them long, that he would come to learn the business and then be off as soon as he could start up on his own. But the two owners, Forest Lowrey and Ward Pearl, were sympathetic: they had started that way themselves.

The American Mineral Spirits Company of Chicago was an ideal nursery for a man with Bob's ambitions. It was a small independent company whose owners had come up the hard way, knew every side of the business and kept in close touch with their employees. For its size its activities were varied, and being small there was little departmentalization. Everybody knew what was going on. As well as refining oil and marketing in locations as far apart as Texas and New York, the company served the paint industry and produced forms of petroleum products for a diversity of commercial purposes. They had offices in New York and Chicago, their own tank cars and a fleet of trucks. Lowrey and Pearl treated Bob as a trainee, taking him on trips to the oil fields and the out-of-town offices. Insofar as he had a definable job it was to sell the various products to a variety of customers and follow up sales with inquiries about service. He stayed with Lowrey and Pearl for two years.

In his last few months there, he began to look around for a small refinery that could be bought cheap. In December 1941, after several disappointing prospects, an approach came from the owners of the Bell Oil and Gas Company, Samuel Lubell and his son Benedict, of Tulsa, Oklahoma. The Lubells already owned two refineries in Oklahoma, which shipped low-priced gasoline to distant and unprofitable markets in the Upper Midwest by tank car. They were now looking for a more remunerative business with markets nearer home. They found it in Artesia, New Mexico—Malco Refining, Inc. (MALCO). The refinery was small, with a capacity of only 1500 barrels a day. The owners of MALCO were willing to sell the refinery because they wanted to concentrate on the production of crude.

The Lubells needed a partner to help them buy and run their new refinery. The MALCO refinery had only modest possibilities, but they were what Bob was looking for. He consulted his father. Hugo Sr. had always wanted to finance something in which his three sons could be partners. Now that they were away from home he felt it more strongly.

The Lubells' proposal was that they and the Andersons would each acquire a half-share in MALCO, each side putting up $150,000—in those days a substantial sum. On December 30, 1941, three weeks after Bob first heard of the Lubells, he became vice president and secretary of MALCO. One of the Lubells' Bell Oil deputies, Ira ("Pop") Anson, was appointed MALCO's president. Two days later, on January 1, 1942, Bob and Barbara, and their baby, Katherine, set out by car on the long journey from Chicago to Artesia, more than a thousand miles as the crow flies.

In 1942, though the fifth largest state in the Union, New Mexico was one of the six least populated, with only half a million residents to its 121,666 square miles, about four persons to a square mile. One quarter of it was wilderness, another quarter forest and woodland; its water area was the smallest in the United States, and most of the state was classified as "semi-arid," with temperatures reaching as high as

116°F. Navajo, Apaches, Utes, Comanches and other Indians made up 10 percent of the inhabitants. Nearly half the population spoke Spanish, the Spaniards having ridden there in 1540 in search of fabled treasure, driving sheep and cattle before them. Space was the key to the life of the state, grazing its economy. The average distance between families was a mile.

New Mexico also had an abundance of oil, coal, copper, silver and gold. Cattle-raising was still the major source of wealth, but the production of energy was soaring. Oil had been discovered near a Navajo reservation in the early twenties—to the disgust of the Indians, who had been searching for water—and at Artesia a few years later. By 1932 New Mexico was a major oil producer. In the early 1940s the University of California built its Scientific Laboratory at Los Alamos. During the war the United States Air Force had extensive training fields there. In 1941, while the Indians in their pueblos were still practicing religious ceremonies thousands of years old, and the descendants of the Spanish empire builders were still dancing to the folk music of the Mexicans, the B-29s, built and fueled by the more recently arrived gringos, roared above their heads.

Barbara had had no idea of what New Mexico would be like. She knew there were deserts and high mountains, and had "a vague idea of . . . sleeping under giant cacti like tourist bookends." Artesia, she found, was a typical Southwestern town of about 4000 inhabitants, with a broad Main Street with small stores on either side, an unpaved section for the blacks and Spanish Americans, and for the rest "many small plastered houses with front and back yards in various states of disrepair, a few gardens with roses, columbine and morning glory." The Andersons found a white stucco house with a picket fence and a garden, and moved in as soon as the furniture arrived. They were in a new world.

Barbara wrote about the character of life in Artesia in the forties:

Most women did their own housework, took care of their yards and gardens, bought, canned and cooked their meals, and many sewed for their homes and families as well. Most had one car used more by their husbands. You had to make your own entertainment. There was no television. One or two nights each week we hired a sitter and went to the one movie, often Saturday, or to a party of four to eight young couples with guests dining in every room, including the bedrooms.

Monday was a day of toil to clean and usually do the washing after a weekend of social or religious activity. Tuesday followed with the family ironing and most women's groups, religious or civic, met on Wednesday afternoon. Choirs rehearsed or political activities took place on Thursday nights so men could participate, and Friday led into another weekend with each small head to shampoo, mending, polishing, etc., for the weekend. We were all very busy, husbands with small businesses and wives with homes and families, in spite of which most of us attended Red Cross First Aid, canning or preserving classes, or took or taught art or music as a hobby or a vocation. Most women drank very little, only at parties, and, with few exceptions, we did not flirt with the husbands of friends. They were friends also. However, males tended to group together in the kitchen talking politics—they might play poker—while their wives sat "dressed up" in the living room, talking of children and wartime shortages, where to buy meat and the best brand of shoes for toddlers. After dinner there might be charades. There was a shortage of doctors so we gave each other medical advice, especially family concoctions for children's coughs or croup, one of which was a teaspoon of kerosene with a lump of sugar dissolved in it.

It was very very hot, and, in those days, there was no cooling system. Bob invented his own. When the family went to bed, he opened all the windows to let in the cool night air. He got up at 4:30 A.M. and closed the windows to trap the cool air in. For his system, the rest of us had nothing but praise, so long as he was the one who got to get up at 4:30.

When the Americans declared war Bob, with his brothers, had reported for duty, but as he was, unlike them, a father, he was sent back to continue his job. Soon after, since he was working in essential industry, he was put in a "deferred" class. "Refineries in those days, forty years ago, were relatively uncomplicated," he recorded, "and because of the recession you could hire plenty of qualified engineers." There were about thirty-five men working in the refinery under the superintendent, Lowell ("Pete") Naylor, who had considerable experience of the industry. The crude oil was extracted about thirty miles away, collected by the gathering lines and pumped into town through the pipeline. At the refinery it was broken up into its simple components—the gasoline fraction, the kerosene fraction, the diesel fraction and so on. Some went into a thermal cracking unit—heat treatment at high temperatures to improve the yield and quality of gasoline—capable of producing a high-octane gasoline which, with the addition of lead, became a premium fuel. Part of the highest octane gas produced by MALCO was suitable for aircraft.

The product then had to be sold. To keep the books and make the sales, there was a small administrative staff housed a block away from the refinery in a rented office in a small brick-fronted building on Main Street which at one time had been a store. Containing the three desks of the bookkeepers of the old MALCO management on the left, and three new desks for the new management on the right, the office was crowded. Bob sat at the desk nearest the door. Joe Lackey, an accountant of about Bob's age, who arrived from Tulsa to represent Bell Oil, sat behind him. Joe Lackey remained in Bob's employ for forty years. "In all that time Joe and I were never much more than a desk apart."

Joe Lackey recalled that in the first three months Bob spent most of his time with Pete Naylor working inside the refinery: "They were at it from early in the morning to late at night. Bob had ideas and a good deal of know-how; Pete was ready to apply them." Bob was convinced that the plant could be made at least twice as productive. "They put in new pieces of equipment, a fractionating column here, a weight tank there, and Bob experimented with temperatures, volumes and mixes to improve the quality and boost the output: in refining that's the key to profitability."

Sometimes Bob made a suggestion and was told: "It's never been tried before." He'd say: "Well, let's try it *now.*" His men entered into the spirit of the thing. They had known for years that the plant was underproducing, that its equipment needed replacing, that its management had not really cared. They liked the new young boss, with his readiness to outwork them all to give the plant new life. They responded. In the first six months output went up from 1500 to 4000 barrels a day. Earnings and profits went up accordingly. MALCO moved out of its rented space in the warehouse and took three rooms in a newly built office block. Bob bought his first company car for $1500. MALCO was on its way. So was Bob Anderson.

Though he had hired a salesman, Bob Anderson never took his own eye off his sales, a habit which has never left him. He soon heard of a most attractive potential customer for his recently increased output of diesel fuel. This was a highly mysterious government installation two hundred fifty miles away, near what had once been a boys' school at Los Alamos. The buildings were located somewhere within a heavily wooded tract reached by a long dirt road. MALCO's diesel trucks were halted at the perimeter, their drivers replaced by authorized personnel; all attempts at conversation were discouraged. According to the gossip in the bars of Santa Fe, this camp was a home for pregnant unmarried Army women, but this hardly explained the vast demand for diesel or the fact that the installation was highly classified. The secret was well kept. Not until three months before the explosion at Trinity Site, White Sands, did Bob Anderson hear from a friend that "a thing called an atomic bomb was being developed at Los Alamos. I instinctively suspected that he was right, but I had no idea how he knew, nor if he really *did* know. I certainly didn't know at this time that some of my old friends at the University of Chicago were highly involved in the production of the missile."

By coincidence Bob and Barbara witnessed the first explosion. They were in their cabin at the Artesia Sacramento Camp in the mountains. One night they arranged to have one of their neighbors, A. C. Sadler, give Bob a lift into town before dawn the following morning. At 5:30 A.M. their room was suddenly lit as though by daylight. Barbara woke at once and said to Bob, "A.C. must be ready to leave now; he's turned his headlights on." Later, over the radio, they heard the government's official explanation: an ammunition dump in the vicinity had accidentally exploded.

More important to MALCO than the increased sale of diesel was Bob's success with high-octane gasoline. When he arrived at MALCO the highest octane rating was 60. "Why so low?" he asked. The answer: "Well, that's what it's always been." This was not good enough for him. The higher the octane, the higher the potential profit if enough could be produced to meet the investment. After some months of re-equipment and experiment, Bob Anderson and Pete Naylor were producing high-octane gas, earning a much higher selling price per gallon. This would have been a valuable gain at any time, but as it happened the circumstances could not have been more propitious. In the town of Roswell, forty miles due south, the Army was expanding its Air Corps bases to meet the demands of war. Their huge Boeings needed 91 octane aviation gasoline. Some of it was being freighted to Roswell from a thousand miles away. MALCO's proximity to the airfields gave it a great opportunity, if it could make it—the shorter the haul, the higher the profit. Bob talked to the Air Corps purchasers, went back to Lackey and said, "Joe, I've got exactly thirty-one days to produce 91 octane and convince the Air Force I can guarantee a permanent supply." They worked day and night. By the early fall, MALCO's trucks were delivering gas to the airfields at 6 cents a gallon, an increased price the operatives never thought to see. This, as well as a sense of directly contributing to the most spectacular part of the nation's war effort, had a great effect on their morale. "But the main achievement was persuading them that it could be done," said Lackey. "Until Bob *showed* them they just didn't believe we could produce 91 octane. That's where Bob's gift of leadership came through. Don't forget he was only twenty-four—two years out of college, working with men who'd been refining crude for twenty and thirty years."

There had been collisions during the first two months of the partnership. The Lubells appreciated Bob's ability and the speedy improvements in the refinery's fortunes, but they had misgivings. "He was going too fast for them," says Lackey, who in his post as the Lubell accountant was in a position to know. "They could see he had his own methods of running the business, which weren't theirs. They were conservative and cautious. Bob was bold and experimental. Above all, he was, and is, a risk-taker, and they knew it. They would never have dared even *try* to make 91 octane gas."

The Lubells had thought that MALCO would be run from their Tulsa office. In the first two months, they pestered Bob with critical telephone calls, and Anson visited MALCO customers, pointedly asking how Bob was "doing." Lackey was flooded with demands for returns and reports he did not have time to supply. Because Bob was—and looked—so young, and was so pleasant and easygoing, the Lubells thought he would do as he was told. They were neither the first nor the last to make that mistake. Two months after his arrival in Artesia, Bob told the Lubells he would run the company his own way or get out. The Lubells gave way. Sam Lubell's nominee, "Pop" Anson, ceased to be president and Bob took his place. Joe Lackey became assistant secretary. Five years later Bob bought the Lubells out, for seven times the original value of their shares. Looking back on those days he says: "The Lubells were fine partners who were more interested in refining than in oil and gas exploration."

In 1942, six months after he became president of MALCO, Bob bought a second refinery, the Valley Refining Company in the town of Roswell. It was even smaller than the Artesian operation, processing only 600 barrels a day, but Bob was convinced that it had much greater potential which he could realize quickly. Valley had relied for its crude on trucking, an expensive operation. Bob decided to construct a forty-mile pipeline which would bring crude from the Square Lake field. He had also decided that Valley was capable of producing high-quality aviation gas, not the 91 octane being made in Artesia, but an 89 octane for use in smaller aircraft—also very profitable. Because the weather was so stable in that part of New Mexico, the Air Force planners had opened several new training bases there. Valley's 89 octane gas was in great demand at the Fort Sumner base only a hundred miles or so away. Once Bob had described the potential to the Lubells, Valley looked a bargain at $100,000. The premises, standing near the New Mexico Military Institute on the east edge of Roswell, became a part of the Anderson history. Expanded and modernized, forty years later it is still Bob's personal base; he sits in the same office he acquired in 1942.

CHAPTER THREE

A wildcatter is an independent oil producer who, at his own expense, explores for oil and gas and, when he thinks he may have found it, drills a well. If he strikes it rich he may make a fortune. If the well is dry he foots the bill. He may drill fifty wells and end up with nothing but his own bankruptcy. He may be lucky the first time. A "producer" well is drilled in the knowledge that a worthwhile field is there. A "wildcat" well is drilled in hope. The wildcatter is to oil what the lone prospector with his burro, pick and pan is to gold. The wildcatter is the greatest risk-taker in the riskiest business ever. Indeed, the risks have sometimes been so extreme that the term "wildcat" is often used to describe an undertaking which sensible men think unsound.

Bob decided the time had come for him to wildcat. He had gone into refining only as the first step to becoming an oil producer. He bought $1400 worth of well-used drilling equipment and hired Harry Steinberger, an elderly man who had worked in the oil fields all his life, to operate it. He also bought Harry's one and only drilling rig and the lease of the land near Roswell on which Harry was currently drilling. Bob was his own chief geologist and decided personally where they would drill. The first five years or so produced one oil field and a succession of mostly dry holes. Undaunted, Bob rode around in his car, frequently taking Barbara with him, studying the ground, observing where other men were striking oil and buying up cheap leases from the government or private individuals. He drilled fifteen wells before he hit the Caprock field.

By 1945, twenty of his wells were producing in the area, but owing to government regulation of output, the yield was small. He could not then afford to go after anything big. Consequently, there were many disappointments during that period. For example, he had spent a great deal of time surveying a prospect at Rangely, in northern Colorado, and concluded it was most promising, but decided to drop the project when he learned that the price was $3 per acre. He felt $3 was more than he could then risk for 30,000 acres. Two years later, a 400 million–barrel oil field was discovered there—the biggest discovery in the Rocky Mountains. When he was asked what he thought about that denouement he laughed and said, "Never look back in this business. If you do you'll lose your nerve."

The end of the war brought changes. The railroad companies abandoned the old oil-burning steam locomotives for the more efficient diesels. Demand for oil fell; the Roswell plant throughput went down nearly 25 percent in a year. Perceiving that though military consumption was declining, civilian demand was growing in the north of the state, Bob decided to increase production at Roswell and offer the Artesia Refinery to the Continental Oil Company (CONOCO) in February 1946. The MALCO staff moved to Roswell.

Valley, as Bob had calculated, was able to meet the demand even though Artesia had been disposed of. Soon after, with things going well, he bought the small Ute oil refinery in Graham, Texas. Hugo Jr. had now been discharged from the Army. Bob persuaded him not to go back to the bank but to come to Texas and manage Ute. Soon after him came Donald, demobilized from the Navy. Donald, a trained engineer, took over the MALCO pipeline system, which was undergoing expansion in line with Bob's policy of cutting costs by using pipelines instead of trucks. MALCO now had its own extensive pipeline system to Roswell. When Caprock began to produce, Bob built a thirty-two-mile, four-inch line from it to Roswell. As the use of pipelines expanded, MALCO formed its own pipeline company under Donald. When it was sold in 1959 it covered 320 miles.

Bob generally started his day by arriving at the refinery by about 8:00 A.M. He and plant manager Joe Whitehurst would go over the previous day's operations—study the yields, the rate of throughput and sales, check oil receipts, look at the inventories. Doing this every day, he knew exactly what was going on in every nook and cranny of the business. If a pump had broken down overnight, they would go and look at it. If a temperature gauge had been repaired, they would go and check it out. Then Bob would go to the office and work through the mail with Joe Lackey. During the war and in early peacetime, there was much government correspondence—forms to fill, regulations to take note of, ration cards, gasoline ratings, various licenses. "Joe and I were always cussing about the red tape," Bob remembered. Then he would talk to the superintendent of the pipelines. There would be many conversations with purchasers. There were problems with the unions, with the state bureaucracy and the government. Frequent changes in specifications and regulations meant changes in the production plan. Bob was in Washington every couple of months to ask for changes or cancellations in instructions, or reductions in paperwork. About once a month he went to Santa Fe, the state capital.

Within the course of a day, innumerable people carrying rolls of maps would come in to offer him deals, partnerships or land leases, or to ask him to drill for them. He was more inclined to say yes than no. "There were some pretty wild, long shots," recalled Joe Lackey, "but Bob took a few." The telephone was always ringing—customers wanting to reorder or asking why the first order had not been delivered. What did Bob and the two Joes talk about most? "Increasing throughput." They doubled it in a year without additional equipment. In the early days, equipment was hard to get; it had gone straight from the factory to the Army, so they could increase their production only by redeploying what equipment they already had and using their wits. To do it Bob read technical books and equipment manuals—"everything he could get his hands on," said Joe. When they could get it, they put in new equipment, often having to modify it themselves to suit their own requirements—modified pumps, modified heating equipment, modified furnaces. "And we had to improvise. Only Bob had the knowledge, and only he had the confidence. It was a one-man band." For Bob it was, as he recorded later, "a unique school."

Bob and Barbara moved from Artesia to Roswell at the end of 1945. For the next twenty years the pattern of their lives did not much change. Roswell in the 1940s, with a population of 13,000, was, compared to Artesia (4000), a metropolis, but its inhabitants were even more scattered, and with its dusty broad street and low buildings along it at wide intervals it looked like a small cow town in a western film. It had sprouted at the junction of the Hondo and Pecos rivers, its gramma grass proliferating around the rare New Mexico water, providing excellent feed as a grazing stop along the route for livestock driven north from the Texas ranges to the military forts of Colorado. In 1880 Roswell had consisted only of a cattle pen, a house and a primitive hotel for trail drivers. It soon became a town of cattle barons, men like the famous John Chisum, "The King of the Cattle Ranchers," who established his headquarters six miles south of the town at the South Spring ranch—now owned by the Andersons.

It was in Roswell, in 1946, that the Andersons began their close friendship with Paul Horgan which has lasted to this day. Horgan, destined to become one of America's most eminent novelists, a Pulitzer Prize–winning historian and a distinguished literary critic, returned to his home in Roswell to resume his career as a creative writer after four years' service in World War II. He soon made the acquaintance of the enterprising young industrialist who had just arrived in town and introduced him to his Roswell friends. Horgan took to the Andersons and their children, and being a bachelor, went there frequently for dinner.

Afterwards, Bob, Barbara and I would go to the library in the house, and they would ask me to read from my current writing. So many, many evenings—I can't tell you how many—I would simply unreel the new story I was writing, or the new chapter of a book or whatever, so I had their ear, their encouragement—their response, which was always extremely valuable to me—and affectionate. It was a cultivated atmosphere.

And this gave me some reassurance because Roswell is not, with all its virtues, particularly centered around this kind of thing. On the whole it was a kind of oasis for me and perhaps for them.

It was a great joy to me as an unmarried person, and without my own children, to be taken that warmly into their circle and to know their children as they grew. All of them I found to be extremely attractive and bright, and generally sweet people. What impressed me always, and to this day impresses me, is the degree to which both Bob and Barbara not only allowed, but encouraged, the children to be individuals. I never saw one example of strain in that family between the parents and the young, and that I thought quite extraordinary. The manner was always informal, always easy, always loving and affectionate, but there was always some marvelous bond of dignity that kept a nice atmosphere between them all. I credit Barbara, probably more than Bob, with the miracle job she did as a parent. I've always felt her to be superbly broad and understanding with each of the children on a completely separate basis. She saw them as they each were individually, and fostered that individuality. I thought this a perfectly wonderful demonstration of how to release human values in young people growing up, and this was consistent.

On the other hand, Bob had with the children a kind of humorous, almost at times comic, tolerance of their individualities, their quips, their eccentricities, their idiosyncrasies, but again very much allowing them to be who they were and how they were. I think particularly with the two boys, whom he saw, as they did eventually, as coming into his world of the businessman—I think he saw the necessity of some kind of endowment for them in training for these jobs in particular ways. They've both worked out well as junior entrepreneurs of the Anderson empire.

A third person joined what Paul Horgan called "a kind of triumvirate"—Peter Hurd, who was to become one of the best known of America's contemporary painters. Horgan said:

Bob took delight in collecting works of art. He had, and has, a definite feeling for them. He liked to paint himself—he called himself "a Sunday painter." I own a couple of pictures which he gave to me. I drew and painted a little—still do upon occasion when I need to make visual notes for what I write—so we had that very much in common. A kind of triumvirate feeling developed between Robert and myself and Peter Hurd. Peter and Robert became enormously close friends, and remain so—I think that has been the closest friendship that Robert has had of which I know. That was the beginning of the triumvirate—all of us to one degree or another being painters—Peter being supremely the professional, myself the amateur for a purpose, and Bob the amateur for simple amusement and delight—but with a real talent. He painted and simply enjoyed the act of feeling the medium of paint as he enjoyed looking at it done by others.

The late forties saw a further drop in the demand for petroleum. The need for military purposes continued to decline, and the new postwar automobile boom had not yet arrived. From 1946 to 1950 MALCO made a number of tactical moves—selling here, buying there, reducing output, switching production, adjusting to the market. Bob found selling as easy as buying: his policy was to buy cheaply a plant which was in need of improvement and management, realize its potential, get it working really efficiently, then sell at an attractive price which would leave him with an acceptable profit.

The period 1949–50 was not a happy one for the American oil industry: a sudden glut of foreign crude precipitated a drastic reduction of refinery output all over the United States. But for Bob the year was golden: he pulled off his first big coup. What later came to be known as the Manning Deal lifted him overnight from the junior league of independent oil producers to the top echelon of the national league. He became famous throughout the American oil industry at the age of thirty-three.

Fred M. Manning was one of the most colorful characters in the oil industry. He was typical of the oil men Bob's father used to talk about when he returned home to Chicago from his trips to Texas and Wyoming. Fred had first earned his crust as a "roughneck"—a laborer on the floor of an oil rig—and later, by skill, knowledge and forcefulness, had become a driller and producer millionaire. His highly valuable oil and gas leaseholds extended from Canada through the Rockies down to Texas. His empire included twenty-three drilling rigs, a fleet of tankers and three airplanes. In 1950 he was only fifty-one, but he was ailing. He knew he should retire, but he could not bring himself to make the decision, and he could not bear to sell. There were two questions to be answered: could Fred be persuaded to sell? And if so, by whom? Many of the biggest oilmen in America were trying to find out.

Ever since he went into the oil business Bob had thought that the Rocky Mountains was a great area for expansion. In 1948 he began to make inquiries. The going was not easy. In all, the negotiations took two years. "Fred was invariably surrounded by half-a-dozen 'advisors,' " Bob recalled many years later. "I found that the only way to get to him was on the telephone." Fred's state of health made him impatient and irascible, and since he did not want to retire, and contemplated it only on account of his ill health, he was frequently stubborn and resentful when the future of his business was discussed, and reacted irritably to lengthy legal conversation. Many potential purchasers gave up trying, or eased off. Bob hung on, and the turning point came when he learned something his competitors did not know: Fred Manning had just bought a home in California, a home obviously meant for retirement. This, Bob calculated, was imminent. He renewed his siege. Fred had taken a liking to this up-and-coming, relaxed young oilman with the easy manner, the open smile, and bow tie and Stetson. He saw Bob as being like himself—a Rocky Mountains man, a risk-taker, a wildcatter. He decided to sell.

Fred and his lawyers met Bob in Denver, the Manning headquarters, at the famous Brown Palace Hotel. Fred's lawyers surprised Bob by presenting him with terms different from those he had agreed with Manning personally. He refused to sign, giving his reasons. He then took a single sheet of the Brown Palace Hotel writing paper and wrote out a contract on one side of it. Fred accepted. (The sheet of notepaper, framed, now hangs on the wall of Bob's Roswell office.) The acquisition gave MALCO a large and diversified exploration base for oil and gas in the Rockies alongside its own now extensive oil and gas holdings. MALCO became a leading Rockies operator. Bob now had a headquarters in Denver as well. The deal was given immense publicity in the oil industry: the $11 million purchase, by a thirty-three-year-old, was considered a remarkable coup. It rated a headline in the *Denver Post* and introduced Bob to the ranks of the nation's major oil producers.

With the major acquisition went four others. The first of these was

John Lyon, Manning's chief pilot. John now became Bob's chief pilot and remained so until he retired thirty-five years later. Flying had already played a large part in Bob's career. He had bought his first plane in 1945, a twin-engine Cessna. Later he switched to a Beechcraft stagger-wing biplane. He had seen that unless he used a plane he could not visit all his sites at sufficiently short intervals. He had already made up his mind that no company, however big or small, could be run from a desk at headquarters. "The chief executive officer must constantly get out into the field and discuss the operational problems with the operators." He also believes that the administrative staff at headquarters must be strengthened from time to time by bringing in men who have had operational experience in the field. "The top men back at headquarters should be men brought in from the field."

Now that he had to travel greater distances in these early Rocky Mountain years he had to use aircraft even more. The three planes that came to him with John Lyon in the Manning deal included a twin-engine Beechcraft biplane. Bob later recounted:

> It was a racing biplane, but it took us three hours to do what we could do in less than an hour today. Even so we traveled far faster than any other means of movement. And traveling by air gave me time to think. Some of the most useful thinking I've done about my business has been in the quiet and seclusion of a flight in an airplane. I couldn't have done what I've done if I hadn't been able to use aircraft. I've spent about 20,000 hours in the air in my lifetime—that's the equivalent of three normal pregnancies. I reckon to fly between 200,000 and 300,000 miles a year.

In his active service John Lyon saw the flotilla of four aircraft grow into a fleet of about thirty-five aircraft, including a dozen jets, two 727s and a 707. There were some accidents, but only one which could have been fatal. In 1957 Bob bought a converted A-26, the Douglas attack bomber. Its two 2500-horsepower engines enabled it to do more than 400 miles an hour at 25,000 feet. It was the fastest propellor-driven plane extant. John Lyon called it "a passenger's nightmare and a pilot's dream," the nightmare for the passenger being the speed at which it landed—"it scared the daylights out of them." Barbara Anderson recalled that when they were due to land at an airport, a crowd of curious onlookers would gather to watch it come in. "I think they were all waiting for it to crash."

A month after it had been purchased, during which time it had not been giving complete satisfaction, the A-26 came in to land at Roswell en route from Los Angeles. As well as John Lyon and Bob Anderson, Mr. and Mrs. Joe Whitehurst were on board. On landing, the plane's right-wing engine burst into flames. The *Roswell Record* reported next day: "Lyon braked the plane to a quick halt, ran it off the runway, and along with the passengers and the co-pilot moved quickly away." The fire brigade and ambulance roared out to meet them. John Lyon's account of it is as follows: "We jumped out of the plane and ran, and we were standing well back when the fire trucks came clanging up. Mr. Anderson, who was not addicted to expletives, said, 'We don't need the fire trucks. Let the son-of-a-bitch burn.' " Later the A-26 was sold to the Phillips Petroleum Corporation in exchange for a large quantity of butane.

The second acquisition from Manning was a two-year-old yellow Oldsmobile convertible which Bob still drives. Its top has never been raised. Snow, thunderstorms and autumn leaves have year by year visited their consequences on the floor and seats. But still the car goes.

The third acquisition was E. W. Bisett, who was to become a close friend of the family. At that time, Ed, a thirty-year-old lawyer, was working in the Land Department of the Manning Company, with responsibility for leaseholds and purchases. He had heard rumors that a firm called MALCO was trying to buy Manning, but had not paid much attention to them. He knew only two things about MALCO. First, that it was much smaller than Manning, which made him skeptical about its chances of an acquisition—"You see, I didn't know Bob"—and that it "had elegant notepaper—far superior to that of any other company I dealt with, functional, but artistic, which, of course, I came to know was Bob's style."

One morning he was asked to go to the office of the company's president. When he got there he was introduced to a Mr. Robert O. Anderson, the president of MALCO, who was about to become the owner of Manning. "What struck me was that he looked so youthful and relaxed to be doing such a big deal," said Ed, "and I saw that he wore a bow tie." With his well-cut business suits, bow tie and Stetson, Bob has the curious effect of impressing easterners as Western and westerners as Eastern, a paradox in appearance which reflects a paradox in his personality. Bob began to question Ed. "He seemed to know a good deal about me already; he led me into the answers, you know: 'I think you went to law school at Harvard, didn't you?' and so forth. Then he asked me if I'd like to work for him in Roswell. 'We can't use you in our Land Department,' he said. 'We have enough people working in it already. But you could work in the Law Department. In fact,' he said, 'you could *be* the Law Department.' " Bisett accepted Bob's offer.

The Manning deal was a great step forward for MALCO and was much noted in the industry. Manning was one of the top ten drilling companies in the world. Acquiring it had catapulted Bob into the ranks of the heavy players. A national journal at the time described MALCO as now having become "a miniature Standard Oil of New Jersey," citing its large income from the production of crude, its many refining operations and its 450,000 acres of undeveloped lease-holdings. These holdings were the key factor to Bob's expansion over the next few years, and the basis of MALCO's policy—to acquire large acreage, and wait for producers on neighboring sites to strike oil and prove MALCO's holdings. The policy required patience and capital. Bob had always had patience, and now the acquisition of Manning provided the capital. This was used to acquire more refining capacity as well as for the purchase of more leaseholds. The following year Bob was appointed to the prestigious National Petroleum Council. At thirty-four, he was the youngest member of the council by sixteen years. (He has continued to serve on the council under eight successive presidents.) The fact that he rose to these heights in the industry while still so young is part of the reason for his power. He has grown up with seven successive chairmen of Exxon. A recent chairman of Exxon, hardly younger than Bob, was an unheard-of geologist in a district office when Bob was the talk of the oil world for bringing off the Manning deal.

Bob's reputation as a risk-taker and go-getter was now widely known. He had no shortage of invitations to join others in wildcatting of one kind or another. Some of these were interesting but dubious. He was asked to make an investment in Sumatra, but declined after discovering that the area was plagued with the activities of Communist guerrillas. Another invitation came from a Guatemalan who asked for $100,000 to be deposited in his name in a bank in Mexico City. To check on him, Bob asked about this person at the U.S. consulate in Guatemala City. Some days later an official at the consulate telephoned Bob to ask if he knew a person (the same one) who claimed to be a business partner of his. That possibility stopped there. Closer to home, an Artesia drilling operator tried to persuade him to invest in a lead and silver mine located in the Sacramento Mountains to the west of Roswell. "It'll be a real money-maker," he assured Bob. "The only impurity we've got to worry about up there is gold."

In 1952 MALCO acquired more plants at Prewitt and Bloomfield in New Mexico, and bought more and more land leases and licenses to drill all over the Southwest. Bloomfield was a perfect example of the MALCO method. "When we bought it," said Joe Whitehurst, "it was just about as primitive a skimming operation as you could have seen, with the still up on bricks, heated by burning the oil leaking from it. The faster it leaked, the more the refining process speeded up. We bulldozed the plant, had a furnace made in Houston, Texas, built a cracking tower from scrap, and jumped the Bloomfield output from 300 to 750 barrels a day." The following year they bought the New Mexico Asphalt & Refining Company (NUMEX) with an output of 5000 barrels a day and a jet fuel contract for the new Walker Air Force Base nearby at Roswell. Whitehurst quickly boosted NUMEX asphalt from zero to 1800 barrels a day. By 1959 the company refinery was selling hot asphalt nearly all over New Mexico, and production had been raised to 12,000 barrels a day.

All these purchases increased MALCO's strength and enhanced Bob's reputation. But the deal which in Joe Lackey's opinion was "the first really big one, the one that proved to me that Bob was going to make the top" was just about to come: the purchase of the nationally known Wilshire Oil Company of California.

In 1950 Bob had picked up a piece of information from an old friend of his, Ed Frazier, who was always on the lookout for acquisitions. Ed mentioned a large refinery located just south of Los Angeles, the Wilshire Oil Company. Despite owning a huge tank farm and three hundred acres of good industrial sites, said Frazier, Wilshire was in difficulties and could be bought cheaply. Bob was just beginning the program of acquisitions described. He had much on his mind, but he stored the information away.

Four years later he was invited to a luncheon party to be given by Arthur Stewart, vice president of the Union Oil Company, on his yacht, anchored in Los Angeles harbor. When Bob arrived in Los Angeles he hired a car to drive him to the harbor, going via Norwalk, the site of Wilshire's refinery, so that he could have a good look at Frazier's tip.

By the time he arrived at the yacht, he had made up his mind what to do. First, he was sure that the plant was worth far more than the $8 million asking price. Secondly, he was sure that the highly competitive West Coast market, plagued by gas wars, had prevented Wilshire from realizing its potential under its present management. Thirdly, he reckoned that the Gulf Oil Corporation (the fourth largest major in the United States) with access to Middle East (Kuwait) crude, would be eager to come into the expanding West Coast market for automobile gas. If so, Gulf might solve the problem of raising the money to purchase Wilshire.

Finally, he believed that he could deal with an all-important problem posed by the nature of Wilshire's ownership. Two thirds of Wilshire was held by a firm of brokers, Blyth and Company, on behalf of the late owner, now deceased; the other third by Mrs. Machris, an elderly widow. The two parties refused to negotiate with each other—each said it could get a better price than the other—but there was a personal element in the impasse, and it was for that reason, he calculated, that all prospective buyers had been refused. Bob thought he might with diplomacy succeed in bringing the two parties together; if he could get both to trust *him,* he could get them to trust each other. He reckoned that Blyth and Company had no wish to run an oil company, and would like to close a deal as soon as possible, take their percentage and get out. As for Mrs. Machris, he hoped he could persuade her to sell. By the time he arrived for lunch at the Stewart yacht he had reached three conclusions: that Wilshire, valued at $8 million, and with a charter on the biggest tanker in the world, the *Universal Leader,* was worth four times as much; that he could persuade Gulf to put up the majority of the funds necessary to make the purchase; and that if she were suitably propositioned, Mrs. Machris would agree to sell.

He set to work. His first move was to arrange the financing of the operation. Gulf was willing to talk to him: his reputation had preceded him, and they did not underestimate their man. They swallowed hard and agreed, as was later recorded in the archives of the Hondo Oil and Gas Company, to "put up a breathtaking 75% of $8 million in return for an agreement with MALCO-Wilshire for the new company to take 20,000 b/d [barrels a day] of Gulf's crude over the next several years." It was also agreed that if MALCO wanted at some future date to sell the Wilshire refinery, Gulf would have the option to buy it.

This part of the deal surprised many of Bob's associates. They knew that he hated preferential rights to buy and had never previously agreed to them: then why had he made an exception in the case of Gulf? After the meeting with Gulf at which he agreed to give them the option, Ed Bisett asked him, "Why did you agree to that?" Bob replied, "Ed, I just made our fortune. I've arranged with them that if I get a good offer I will refer it to Gulf, and that if they don't want me to accept that offer I will have a year to peddle it around at the same price or higher. Gulf won't let me peddle the company around for a year; they'll buy, at my price." Hearing this, Ed Bisett said to himself, Bob, the eternal optimist. But, Ed said later, "Bob turned out to be quite right."

Once he had the necessary funds at his disposal, Bob tackled the problem of persuading the owners to sell. For some years Mrs. Machris had avoided contact with prospective buyers, sheltering herself behind a team of attorneys, who in turn became increasingly difficult to reach. The brokers who owned the other two thirds of the refinery knew how difficult it was for them to talk serious business with prospective purchasers when they were tied down by Mrs.

Machris's veto, so they, too, were not eager to meet prospective clients. Bob, who unlike many great tycoons, revels in personality situations, divined, as it turned out correctly, that while the brokers, the majority shareholders, were ready to get rid of the company, Mrs. Machris, the minority shareholder, was disinclined to appear merely to acquiesce in a majority decision. "It wasn't a matter of price," said Joe Lackey. "That was the mistake some of the others made. It was a matter of psychology. The other buyers had gone about it in the wrong order. They went to the majority stockholder first and Mrs. Machris second. Bob wooed the widow *first.*"

He wrote letters to her and gave telephone messages to her lawyers, as though she, and only she, owned Wilshire, and as though she, and only she, understood its potential and its value. Eventually she asked him to her house. She was wearing an elegant dress made of white leather, over which, putting out his hand to take a proffered Scotch, Bob somehow spilled the drink. After his glass had been refilled, Mrs. Machris continued to listen. He told her that he could offer her a sound financial arrangement, and that he was sure that if she agreed to it, the majority shareholders would go along with it. He pointed out that the partnership he had concluded with Gulf would give Wilshire a new life. He also pointed out that in view of the competition in California, and the vulnerability of a refining operation not supported by co-partnership with a national company wishing to dispose of crude, the existing opportunity for a good sale might not come again. Mrs. Machris decided to sell. The majority shareholders agreed to follow her lead. Bob became the chairman of MALCO WILSHIRE.

Two years after the deal, Wilshire had become the largest independent refiner and marketer in California, and one of the largest in the United States. Bob had become a national oilman, and his personal success in bringing off, on such favorable terms, a deal which had so often been written off as impossible made him a national figure. At forty years of age he was an oil tycoon.

CHAPTER FOUR

Bob's feat of putting together the multimillion-dollar Wilshire deal in California under the noses of the great national companies had, according to *Fortune* magazine, taken him overnight to "an estimated fourth place among U.S. independent refiners," with an annual gross of nearly a hundred million dollars, making him one of the largest independent refining operators in the United States. But just as impressive as the magnitude of his new corporation was the skill with which he had brought it about. Rod Rood, later to become political advisor to Atlantic Richfield, was in those days working for the Richfield company in Los Angeles. "At the time he bought Wilshire," Rod recorded, "I'd not only not met him, I'd never even heard of him. But he changed all that in twenty-four hours. He was obviously a whizz kid. In fact, not only was he a whizz kid, he was different. I went to a lunch he was to attend just after the Wilshire deal just to see what he looked like. He looked very young and relaxed. He didn't look a bit like a tycoon." And he didn't behave like a typical one. "Wilshire had a chain of filling stations," said Ed Bisett. "Bob thought they should have a new logo. He got Herbert Bayer, formerly of the Bauhaus, to design it. He thought that Herbert's designs were splendid, and that all the stations should be repainted to a new aesthetic color scheme. This scheme was to include a special shade of blue to be called 'Bayer blue.' On his first business trip to Wilshire, he took time out to inspect the first repainted filling station. He thought the blue was not the right shade. On three successive trips, he revisited the filling station. He had the blue repainted three times, until they got it right."

On his fortieth birthday, April 13, 1957, Bob was fishing in the Pacific from a boat he had hired for the weekend out of Kona, Oahu, in the Hawaiian Islands. He had flown to Hawaii with the intention of clinching a deal which he had been negotiating for some time—a large property some twenty miles out of Honolulu, called Barbers Point, where he planned to build the refinery and tank farm he had begun to think about when he concluded the Wilshire deal. He had the option and was enthusiastic about it. The aftermath of the Suez crisis and the nationalization of the Suez Canal by President Gamal Abdel Nasser of Egypt nine months before had created an extra demand for American oil which, in turn, had brought about a reduction in the availability of American domestic crude. The major West Coast refineries were on short supply. The vast Pacific Rim would be a lucrative market. Bob intended to exploit it with oil refined at Barbers Point from crude shipped in from the Middle East. The prospects looked good.

Bob arrived in Honolulu late on Friday night. Since there would be no business done over the weekend, he chartered the cruiser *Kona Kai* and sailed out to fish for marlin. For the first two hours there was no sport. Sitting patiently waiting for the fish, leaning back in the stern of the *Kona Kai,* Bob began to ruminate. First he thought about the wonderful prospects opened up by Barbers Point, but gradually, as the waters of the Pacific showed no sign of marlin, he began to ask himself where, "come to think of it," Barbers Point would figure in the ascending curve of his fortunes. From there his mind moved to the fundamental question of where exactly his fortunes were taking him—and his family. It was the thought of the family that caused him to make an important decision. In his own words:

There I was, sitting in the stern of that boat, waiting for a marlin, and, suddenly, all I could think about was the scale of the U.S. inheritance taxes. MALCO was set up legally and financially before I had either a large family or a large business. I knew that if we went into the Barbers Point project we would be going into competition with the really big boys. If you start in that league there's no turning back, and plenty of headaches on the way. Also, I'd been thinking for some time that it might be time to get out of the refining business. It was getting too complicated: too many petrochemicals, too much automation, too much new equipment. Here I was, on my fortieth birthday. The corporation was based on my lifetime. If I got run over by a truck, the tax man would leave only a limited amount for a wife and seven children and many loyal employees, some too old to get a job when I had gone. It came home to me, sitting there on that boat, that it was just foolish to go on as I was.

As his train of thought came to its logical end, a marlin took the bait. In the first few seconds, it was clear that this was a very big fish. After an exciting struggle lasting forty-five minutes, Bob landed it. It was 370 pounds. "A pretty good day's work," said Phil Parker, the skipper. "I think so, too," said Bob ambiguously, his mind on his musings as well as on the marlin. "Let's head back to Kona." On Monday he announced that he would not proceed further with the negotiations for Barbers Point and surrendered his option. In the next two weeks, he pondered on how he would implement the broad decision he had arrived at sitting in the stern of the *Kona Kai*. A month later he initiated plans for the sale of Wilshire Oil, at the best possible price, to the Gulf Oil Corporation.

Ed Bisett recalls that the sale of Wilshire showed an interesting side of Bob as a negotiator: "On this occasion he earned himself a million dollars in one minute." Bob came into Bisett's office and said, "Ed, I'm going to sell the Wilshire company." Ed: "How much are you going to ask for it?" Bob: "I'm going to ask for $25 million and come down a million." The meeting that was to determine the price of the sale took place a few minutes later in Bob's office. It was soon over. Bob came back into Ed's office looking pleased. "How much did you settle for?" Bisett asked. "$26 million." Ed said, "How the hell did you get $26 million when you were only going to ask for $25 million?" Bob said, "Well, a minute before the meeting began, it occurred to me that it would sound better if I came down $2 million instead of $1 million; coming down just $1 million might sound mean. So I started at $26 million, and before I could come down, the price was accepted."

The sale of Wilshire was made to Gulf in February 1958. In the sixteen years since he had arrived in Artesia in 1942, Bob had taken his "listening post," as he had originally conceived the purpose of being in refining, to the very top of the U.S. independent oil industry. This transaction was the beginning of the end of Bob's activities as a refiner. He now owned only one refinery, and that was to be sold before the year was out.

Bob had bought the New Mexico Asphalt & Refining Company (NUMEX) five years earlier, in 1953. At that time the old Valley refinery was showing its age. An investment of some hundreds of thousands of dollars would have been required merely to modernize it. Rather than rebuild, Bob decided to dismantle it, retain the Roswell site as the firm's administrative and bookkeeping headquarters, and buy a larger refinery nearby. One was located near Artesia, NUMEX, owned by a group of Texans led by a famous former football star, Rags Mathews. Its modern plant included a catalytic cracking unit; its output, 5000 barrels a day, was higher than Valley's, and it had a lucrative jet fuel contract to supply the nearby Walker Air Force Base. At the time of the deal, NUMEX, in spite of its title, did not produce any asphalt, and did not need to, but this was soon to change as a result of a change in the market for fuels. Locomotive engines were rapidly being replaced by diesel engines. This led to a reduction in the demand for heavy fuels and an increase in the demand for diesel. NUMEX produced a great deal of heavy fuel but there was no market for it. It was essential to switch production to what was marketable in the changed conditions. "It's got to be asphalt," said Bob. And asphalt it was.

The resourceful Joe Whitehurst was summoned to the helm. He converted NUMEX from fuel to asphalt. Starting from zero, he quickly boosted NUMEX asphalt production to 1800 barrels a day. Bob signed a contract with a Texas-based trucking firm, Ferguson-Steere, to deliver asphalt to customers the length and breadth of New Mexico. He negotiated another remunerative contract with Spencer &

Company of Santa Fe. Spencer had a lucrative business of supplying asphalt to the state's highway department. Within three years, the state of New Mexico's highway department was purchasing more than half a million barrels of asphalt a year for road construction. NUMEX's output went up to 12,000 barrels a day. For the next few years, NUMEX and asphalt looked a very good thing. But by the summer of 1958, circumstances had changed again, and things were looking bad for NUMEX. The demand for asphalt was holding up, but demand for its big by-products was going down fast. Newly designed, high-compression automobile engines were rapidly creating a need for more sophisticated gasolines which NUMEX could not supply. Time to do something, Bob decided. He began to look around for a good buyer, but before he could find even a prospect, events occurred which for a different reason forced upon him the urgent necessity to divest himself of NUMEX: the relationship between NUMEX and Spencer & Company became an explosive issue in New Mexico state politics. The state of New Mexico accused NUMEX of exercising a monopoly in asphalt.

"Fats" Spencer, the owner of the firm which bought the asphalt produced by MALCO and sold it to the State Highway Department, had died of a heart attack in early 1958. His widow decided to sell the business at once. The best bid came from MALCO and Mrs. Spencer accepted it. Nine months later, the newly elected Democratic governor, John Burroughs (Anderson was a well-known Republican), indicted NUMEX on the charge that through its associate, Spencer, it was profiting by a monopoly in asphalt within the state.

It was true that NUMEX was currently the only supplier of asphalt in the state of New Mexico, but there was nothing to prevent anybody else from going into the asphalt business. No objection had been made by the state when MALCO had bought Spencer & Company nearly a year before; the existence of a monopoly was not alleged until January 1, 1959, the day on which the new governor began his term of office. Very soon afterwards, a new asphalt-producing firm, Thunderhead Oil & Gas, announced its existence, and the governor announced that Thunderhead would bid for the state asphalt contracts to come up in April. The governor also announced that in view of the monopoly charges which had been laid against MALCO he would continue to refuse to consider bids from that company for the renewal of its contracts.

In the next few weeks, local newspapers reported that the new Thunderhead Oil & Gas Company's only assets consisted of a dilapidated abandoned garage and an empty 1000-gallon gas tank. The local press also reported that if Thunderhead secured the state contracts, in order to fulfill them it would have to import—at a loss—considerable supplies of asphalt from an Oklahoma firm owned by influential Democrats. Further newspaper reports predicted that the price of asphalt supplied by Thunderhead to the state of New Mexico would in the short term rise by anywhere up to 30 percent. (This turned out to be the case for the next two years.) A newspaper in Albuquerque, the largest city in the state, reported that the new Thunderhead company was owned by friends of the new governor.

Bob Anderson was disgusted. He felt that the charges against MALCO were false and absurd, and that only an abuse of political influence had enabled them to be brought. On May 1, 1959, he leased the NUMEX plant to the Continental Oil Company. He also sold the MALCO trademark and one hundred fifty miles of MALCO pipeline outright. Three months later MALCO Refineries as a company, and as a logo, disappeared. From now on his company in New Mexico, concerned not with the refining but with the discovery and production of oil and gas, would be the Hondo Oil and Gas Company. The Hondo Oil and Gas Company of Roswell was to become Bob's business headquarters, and its emergence was a turning point in his life and career. As he had intended, when the time was ripe he had moved out of refining into production.

This was, of course, not the first time that Bob Anderson had attempted to produce oil. Already in the 1940s there had been the acquisition of several wells—"Nothing to write home about," as Bob said, "but they were producing." It went on this way for a good decade or so: not spectacular, not great, but steady progress—until a breakthrough came in 1957.

This was the discovery of the Empire-Abo field, one of the largest fields in the Permian Basin, itself one of the largest oil-producing areas in the United States, dormant since the leases had been acquired fifteen years previously in 1942. The Empire-Abo was a monument to Bob's long-term policy of the waiting game. Its story is a curious one, illustrating the ups and downs, the freaks of luck and circumstances, with which the history of oil production abounds. Bob had drilled in the Abo field as soon as he acquired it in 1942, but his original well, a shallow one, which he called MALCO State A-1, was not productive. He remained convinced there was oil in the area and continued to buy up land and leases. A few years later he was encouraged in his belief when a firm called Standolind, which belonged to the giant Standard Oil Company of Indiana, discovered oil a few miles southwest of MALCO State A-1. Bob, ever his own chief geologist, studied his state charts and made several inspections of the terrain between MALCO State A-1 and the well which Standolind was now working successfully. He concluded that there was a reef connecting the two, the Abo reef. Some of his existing land and leases were on or very close to it, including the old, dry MALCO State A-1. In 1951, on the hunch that MALCO State A-1 was near the reef, he sent a drilling crew to deepen the old dry well.

The crew deepened the well, and at five thousand feet, having found nothing, paused, and sent for experts to collect and analyze cuttings to see if it was worth drilling deeper. The experts, from a Baroid Well-Logging Service Company, arrived a day late. Not wishing the drilling team to stand idle for a day—drilling was becoming an increasingly expensive operation—its boss decided they might as well use the day's delay to go deeper down. When the experts arrived twenty-four hours later, therefore, they were asked to analyze cuttings taken from the new bottom. They found nothing significant to report. To make sure, the crew drilled a few more hundred feet. The cuttings from this new bottom were analyzed. Again, there was nothing to report. Everybody went back home. Had they known it, on the evening on which they paused, to wait for Baroid, they had drilled into the extreme edge, very thin at that point, of the huge and fabulous Abo pool. If they had waited for Baroid, instead of drilling on down, the cuttings at that level would have shown that the pool was right there. By drilling one more day, they went down through the shallow margin of the pool, and by the time Baroid arrived and took cuttings, they were well into the barren rock below.

Six years later, in 1957, some of Bob's associates advised him to give up the Abo. But he was still sure that the pool was there. By now Standolind was ready to buy Bob out. Bob agreed to let Standolind have some of his acreage in the Abo area, in return for: Standolind undertaking all the costs of exploration; MALCO to pay an agreed share of these costs only if the drilling was successful and led to production; MALCO's share of the expense to be repaid out of the production revenue when that became available. This suited him well: exploration costs were escalating tremendously. He retained the land where he thought the oil was likely to be and sold the acres which he thought least promising. It was all the same to Standolind; they were eager to take anything that was offered. The deal was considered a master stroke.

Before 1957 was out, Standolind had hit the jackpot. Fifteen years after Bob had sunk MALCO State A-1, and six years after the near-miss at the northern edge, the Standolind crew drilled into what was obviously a very wide and deep pool. During the next two years, six other companies owning leases in the area came in to drill. By the middle of 1959, it was clear that the Empire-Abo field was one of the largest fields in the Permian Basin: a quarter-billion-barrel reserve of crude oil. Bob's theory had been proved correct.

By 1962 there were nearly 300 wells in the field, of which MALCO owned 50 outright and more than 100 in part. Bob's waiting game had paid off. Within a year or two of having become a top refiner he had become a top producer of crude. His policy of acquiring a large supply of leases, nursing them, hanging on to them patiently, then encouraging and helping somebody else to prove them, had borne fruit. So had his policy of going it alone. As a wildcatter, unlike most independent producers, he had rarely if ever sold to, or taken in, an outside interest. He preferred to remain a loner.

The widely acclaimed discovery of the Empire-Abo oil field put Bob under a spotlight. Many people were paying attention to this versatile rising star, and none more so than the Atlantic Refining

Company of Philadelphia, the oldest refining company in the United States, founded in 1876. Atlantic was initially interested not so much in Bob as in Hondo. To the board of Atlantic, urgently in need of obtaining more crude, the valuable properties which Hondo held, particularly the still unexploited land and leases which Bob had retained at the time of the deal with Standolind, looked most attractive.

The Atlantic Refining Company, as it was in 1962, had come into existence as a result of the decision made by the Supreme Court in 1911 which found that the Standard Oil Company, of which Atlantic was a subsidiary, had been operating contrary to the antitrust laws of the United States and therefore had to be broken up. As a result of the Court's ruling a number of refining operations were taken from Standard Oil and put into Atlantic. The first head of the restructured Atlantic was Standard's former refining chief, John Van Dyke, who decided that the company should now not only refine oil but move into the service station business, sell oil at the pump and organize a transportation company to make deliveries. By the early 1920s, Van Dyke had realized that to make the refining and pump operation viable, Atlantic would have to produce its own crude. It began to do so and throughout the thirties it built up a big stake in crude production. The majority of its wells were in Oklahoma, Louisiana and, above all, Texas; the headquarters of the production department were in Dallas. By the early sixties, Atlantic was producing a large amount of crude, but not nearly enough.

The Atlantic men in Dallas were able, energetic and successful. They discovered a good deal of oil, developed the fields, and recruited first-class technologists from universities and technical colleges. But the heart and mind, and the power, of the company remained in Philadelphia, in refining and even more in marketing. Commercially the orientation of the two parts of the whole were different. As Bob Anderson put it some years later, "There's often a difference in perspective in the oil industry and it can be very dangerous. Some oilmen are nozzle-oriented; they think the oil industry begins in the filling station, at the pump. Others are well-oriented; they think the industry begins at the well. The proper perspective is to look at the industry as a whole, from well to pump, from start to finish, not at one end or the other."

This was precisely what the Atlantic board in Philadelphia had failed to do, and their failure had been costly. They had not faced the fact that if they did not provide themselves with a greater supply of crude they might have to go out of business. To the source from which greater access to crude might easily be obtained they were relatively indifferent. The board looked on its operation "out" in Dallas much as an early nineteenth-century merchant bank in London might have looked on one of its trading stations "out" in India. Hardly any member of the board made a visit to Dallas—it was much too far away for them. The chairman of the Atlantic board at the time, Henderson Supplee, said jocularly some years later, "I wouldn't have gone across the street to see another oil well. I wouldn't have known what I was looking at." He had spent most of his earlier business life in a milk company owned by his family. Though an extremely able man, Supplee knew little about the oil industry, and did not claim to. Not only did the Atlantic directors in Philadelphia avoid making visits to Dallas, they also did not encourage the Dallas executives to come to Philadelphia.

In spite of the discouragement, one of the Dallas men made the journey to Philadelphia frequently. He was Dow Hamm, an energetic and dedicated oilman in charge of exploration and production. He went to Philadelphia to try to get the Atlantic directors to let him have more money to find more crude. When the directors gave him permission, which was the exception rather than the rule, he returned to Texas and put his proposals into effect. When the board refused to support him he turned a blind eye, went back home and put his proposals into effect anyway, saying nothing. "It was just as well he did," said Bob, looking back twenty years later. "If Dow hadn't surreptitiously broken the rules, Atlantic would probably not have survived."

By 1956 Henderson Supplee and his board had come to the conclusion that Atlantic's future was so limited that something would have to be done if the company was to avoid serious trouble. Significantly, Supplee continued to see Atlantic's problem as one of finance and administration rather than of production—of running the company more efficiently rather than of finding and refining more crude and selling more gas. The vice president in charge of administration and finance was soon to retire. Supplee decided to create a new post, financial vice president, and to look around for a suitable person to fill it. After many months of fruitless searching, Supplee made inquiries at the Harvard Business School. He learned that one of its former associate professors, now a partner in a management consultant firm, was proposing to change his job and might be interested: Thornton Bradshaw.

As it turns out, Bradshaw was to loom very large in the affairs not only of Bob Anderson and Atlantic, but of the business community as a whole. He would become Bob's close personal friend and valued associate, and would serve for seventeen years as the president of ARCO (the conglomerate that was to grow out of Atlantic and its future partner, the Richfield Oil Corporation), seeing the company through some serious difficulties. During this time, he would also occupy a number of distinguished public positions. And in 1981, following a rapid and demoralizing turnover of leadership, the board of RCA would ask Bradshaw to become its chairman and CEO, in hopes of stabilizing its then-precarious situation. Bradshaw would win general praise for his success in turning around RCA and its major asset, the NBC television and radio network, and for negotiating RCA's favorable merger with General Electric.

Supplee interviewed Bradshaw, was impressed and offered him the post. Bradshaw, however, turned the job down, not because of the pay and prospects (Supplee had made it clear that he expected Bradshaw to succeed him as chief executive in time) but because he suspected that "Atlantic was anchored in the past and had no vision of the future." Still, Bradshaw had been very taken with Henderson Supplee—"a splendid gentleman, such a straightforward person, such a good thinker . . . and with such a great sense of social responsibility"—and when Supplee continued to press him Bradshaw changed his mind and finally accepted the post.

It did not take him long to realize that his forebodings were justified. "Atlantic was dead in the water," he recorded many years later. "It had a lot of good professional people in it, but in Philadelphia it had no real leadership." Supplee could not control his executives, and they feuded with each other. "There was bickering at the top level," said Bradshaw. "There being no strong hand at the top level, the vice presidents of the manufacturing, marketing, research and development, and production departments were constantly fighting among themselves. Their battles were not being adjudicated, and each tended to go off in his own direction. A considerable number of personal animosities rose up."

Bradshaw had been recruited to solve a problem, but he saw at once that a far greater one hung like a cloud over the company's head: Atlantic was still producing only half the crude it required; the rest had to be purchased from other companies at any price they cared to impose. It was essential for Atlantic to procure a sufficiency of its own crude immediately, which meant acquiring a company already rich in crude, and integrating that production of crude with manufacturing and marketing in a reorganized and properly directed organization.

One of the obstacles in the way of achieving this, Bradshaw could see, was that Atlantic was no longer one company but two, which were incompatible with each other: the one in Philadelphia and the one in Dallas. "Indeed, there were *five* companies," said Bradshaw, "because each of the three departments in Philadelphia behaved as though *it* was the company, and the executives were at each other's throats." In the City of Brotherly Love the official emphasis was on stability and consolidation; out in Dallas it was on expansion. In Philadelphia were the conservative businessmen, and the ambience was of the sophisticated East; in Dallas were the young Turks who found the oil, and the atmosphere was that of the frontier. The Atlantic men in Philadelphia wore Brooks Brothers suits; the Atlantic men in Dallas wore Stetsons and greeted each other with "Hi!" The executives in Philadelphia seemed hardly ever to talk about oil; the men in Dallas talked of nothing else. "Most conversations in Dallas were full of oil jargon," said Bob Anderson. "The guys in Philadelphia wouldn't have known what the words meant." In Dallas, in spite of the frustrations, and because of Dow Hamm's covert enterprises, there was an atmosphere of excitement. In Philadelphia, in Bob's words, "the only excitement in the day was catching the 5:15 home."

By 1962 Bob Anderson had become a major figure in the oil world. The Empire-Abo discovery had shown him to be one of the most gifted explorer-producers in the United States. The series of MALCO successes had shown his acumen as a refiner, and the Wilshire deal had displayed his skill as a dealer. With Bradshaw's encouragement, Dow Hamm, accompanied by the treasurer in Philadelphia, Lou Ream, went to see Bob in Roswell and asked him if he would consider a merger with Atlantic. Bob said he might. He did not mention that he had been eyeing Atlantic for some time with a view to merging, that he thought its stock was undervalued, that it was not properly run, that it could be turned around and made very profitable. A few weeks before Hamm and Ream came to see him he had had a conversation with Gaylord Freeman about the idea of merging with some other company. "I've gone about as far as I can with Hondo," Bob said. "I'm going to merge with a big one." "Good," said Gaylord, "I've been looking around the big companies. Some of them have problems, but Exxon hasn't. Exxon is the best place for you to go." Bob said, "Gayle, you don't understand. I'm not looking for the *best* place to go, I'm looking for the *worst*. That's where I'll get the biggest percentage to come in with them."

As a result of the meeting between Bob, Dow Hamm and Lou Ream, Atlantic and Hondo began to negotiate. All went smoothly. The day came when it was necessary for Bob to go to Philadelphia to close the deal. He was invited to lunch with Supplee and Thornton Bradshaw at the Racquet Club, one of the oldest and most exclusive clubs in the United States. Bradshaw remembered the meeting in the Racquet Club very clearly. "I can see Bob coming in through the front door wearing his Stetson. I'm sure that was the first time a rancher's hat was ever seen in the cloakroom of the Racquet Club." The three of them talked over lunch. "It wasn't exactly a strained meeting," recalled Bradshaw, "because Anderson and Supplee had one thing in common: they were gentlemen and very considerable persons. But apart from that they were very, very different. Henderson Supplee had never dealt with anybody like Bob before. It was not a matter of dislike or disapproval: Henderson just did not have any ground on which he could meet Bob."

The lunch was merely for the ratification of the treaty: the terms had already been drawn up. Atlantic would trade $32 million worth of Atlantic stock in return for ownership of the Hondo Company and all its assets. Anderson would be invited to join the board of Atlantic. Supplee would continue to be president of the company and chief executive; Bob would become chairman of the Executive Committee; Bradshaw, who had now become executive vice president, would remain in that position—a year later he became president. As a result of the merger Bob would own more of Atlantic's stock than any other single shareholder. "And that for the time being was that," said Bradshaw. "But more was to come."

From that moment people in middle management out in Dallas became aware that things had changed, and for the good. Twenty years later Bill Kieschnick, then president of Atlantic Richfield, recorded how he had felt as a young manager out in Dallas:

> I began to feel that our division was having an easier time selling programs we believed in to Philadelphia. Not everything we put up was adopted, but we now felt that anything we recommended had a really good chance. There was now, obviously, a real intention, a real wish, to develop production of oil and gas. In a word, we felt that our side of the business and at our level was being better understood at the top.

From the beginning of his association with Atlantic, Bob went to Philadelphia frequently and regularly to attend meetings of the board and to offer such advice as his colleagues asked him for. Said Bradshaw, "He listened carefully, but initiated nothing, not until events forced him to. Atlantic was making only meager returns on its investments and had few prospects for improvement. It became more and more clear to the board in Bob's first year on it that the key to Atlantic's movement to improved profitability was production of its own crude. And Bob was not only the sole production man on the board, he was famous for his success at it."

Henderson Supplee either did not see the need for an increase in the production of crude or, seeing it, would not, or could not, do anything about it. By the end of 1964, therefore, the directors of Atlantic, while not relinquishing their respect and affection for their old friend and colleague, came to the conclusion that in the interests of Atlantic Supplee must hand over the reins to a new chief executive. "An interesting story," reflected Bradshaw. "Though they were very gentlemanly, those men were not afraid to act on the facts when they saw them. They put their responsibilities above their personal and social loyalties. They saw that Bob Anderson was not cast in their mold. But they saw that he was the man who could save their company."

When their decision was put to Supplee he resisted it because he sincerely believed that what Atlantic needed was not what Anderson could give. "He simply could not understand," said Bradshaw, "why a good hundred-year-old Philadelphia firm should be committed to a cowboy who had only just arrived in town, how anybody thought the business could be run by a man who had not been tested and evaluated in Philadelphia over several decades." But in early 1965 his old and candid friends on the board, all the stronger because like him they were members of the Philadelphia establishment, finally prevailed upon him to give up the chief executive office.

The particular issue which precipitated the showdown was the imminent retirement of Dow Hamm. Supplee announced that he intended to replace him with an executive from Philadelphia. Bob objected. He said that in his view the Philadelphia man was not the right man for the job, and that since there were better qualified men in Dallas, the appointment would depress morale out there. And Dallas, Bob said, was the key to Atlantic's survival. The board decided to back Anderson. Supplee at once resigned as chairman and chief executive officer, but continued to serve as a director. The board immediately appointed Anderson to replace him, with Bradshaw remaining as president.

"There's no doubt in my mind," said Bradshaw, "that Bob was not at all happy about these developments. First, he did not like the speed and the manner in which Henderson was relieved of his responsibilities. Secondly, he was unhappy about becoming involved in Atlantic to a degree he had never anticipated and had never wanted. He had known, of course, when he negotiated the merger that he would have to give a lot of attention to Atlantic's affairs, but he had thought of that as short-term. He had put a great deal of his personal fortune into the company, and he had to protect it. But he saw all this as a turnaround situation. He hadn't even bought a house or apartment in Philadelphia. He and Barbara had decided to take a suite at the Barclay Hotel for a year and put the two youngest children, whom they'd brought with them, in the Benjamin Franklin Friends Select School for that year. He'd no intention of giving up family life on the ranch in Roswell, and he wasn't aiming to give up his interests in politics to run an oil company on the East Coast. I'm sure as I could be that when the Atlantic board asked him to take over the helm in 1965 it came to him as a surprise, and an unwelcome one at that. But he felt he had no choice."

So, in 1965, less than two years after Hondo merged with Atlantic, Bob became chairman and chief executive officer of Atlantic Refining, and based himself in Philadelphia. The first thing he did in his new job was to "charter a Sabreliner and visit every office in the company. Most of them had never seen a chief executive officer before. Some of them didn't know what a chief executive officer was. But they all seemed pleased to see me. I was made welcome, wherever I went, sometimes before I got there. I got a call from Calgary: they asked me, 'What size hat do you wear?' I said, 'Hell, I don't know, I keep trying them on till I find one that fits. Why do you want to know?' They said, 'We want to give you a Stetson when you get here.' They did too. A huge one, like Tom Mix used to wear." As Bradshaw recalled, "In no time at all, it was clear that Bob Anderson was the boss."

But had Bob believed that the problems of Atlantic could be solved simply by a change of chairman, he would soon have found himself mistaken. Once the internal difficulties had been dealt with, Atlantic felt the full blast of pressures coming from outside. Notwithstanding the new driving force in Philadelphia and the surge of energy and initiative in Dallas, Atlantic found itself up against intense competition from its rivals. "The nub of it," said Bradshaw, "was that Atlantic, though it had a decent marketing base and a decent refining base also, continued to be very weak on production. We still produced less than 50 percent of our crude, and we had no chemical production whatsoever. Whenever the price of crude went up we were whipsawed." The big companies were international, and therefore had unlimited access to cheap foreign crude which they could sell at what price they chose to domestic American companies. In the late fifties the advent of the supertanker, which could bring in vast amounts of crude oil from the Middle East at relatively low cost, had adversely affected the market for domestic producers. Their situation became more difficult when the big companies reached the point at which they had more crude than they could use, and went in for the policy of "monetarizing": knowing that the supply of crude would not last forever they brought as much of it as they could into the States and sold it at the lowest possible price to their own refineries, which were therefore able to sell their gas at the filling station at much lower prices than other retailers. "Atlantic was being doubly hit," said Bradshaw. "We had to buy crude at their prices, and we had to sell gas at their prices. If we were to have a future, somehow we had to break out of that circle; otherwise we'd have to sell out or go bankrupt. This situation had existed *before* we bought Hondo. Indeed, the purchase of Hondo had been intended to help solve the problem. Louis Ream and I had approached damn nearly every oil company in the United States with proposals of marriage. But we had always been rejected. One reason had been that we hadn't enough cash flow to impress the brides. But now, in 1965, that situation had got a lot worse for us."

A few weeks after Bob took charge as chief executive, therefore, the company found itself at the beginning of another, and unprecedentedly bitter, price war. Swift action was necessary if the company was to survive as an independent. Bob began to look around for a company with which a merger would be viable and profitable.

In August 1965, Bob and Bradshaw flew from New York to London to investigate the possibilities of a merger with Belgium Petrofina. The flight did not bring about a merger, but it bore fruit that became much more important. On the way over they discussed the future of

Atlantic. Bob took an envelope out of his pocket and made notes. He wrote down a six-point program which would make Atlantic both the best oil company, professionally, in the world, and big enough to compete with the major companies. First, Atlantic must in time become able to produce for itself all the crude that it needed. Secondly, for the time being it must build a refining and marketing structure sufficiently profitable to enable it to buy crude oil from the major companies, which could exploit the market as a result of the cheap crude they could bring in from their foreign fields. Thirdly, it must build a petrochemical business. Fourthly, Atlantic must be able to supply fuels other than oil, since the oil age might come to an end. The fifth objective was international: to invest in any oil operation within Atlantic's capability which might make a profit. The final objective was to get into other natural resources, such as hard minerals, copper, aluminum, forest products and so forth.

All this meant a tremendous broadening of Atlantic's policy. And it meant that Atlantic must set out to become a much larger company. Objective one, to get all the crude required, meant a reversal of policy. Atlantic had been pump-oriented. Now it was to be well-oriented; it must concentrate on production first and on all stages from then on. This huge change meant a huge risk. And it pointed to the need for a fresh, and more urgent, attempt to merge with another company. These six points, said Bradshaw fifteen years later, became at once the bible of the company and remained so.

On the West Coast, with headquarters in Los Angeles, was the Richfield oil company. Skilled in finding new oil, Richfield produced a great deal of crude. Its exploration had been bold, much of its most recent finds being in Alaska. In 1957 it had discovered the highly valuable Swanson River field, the first commercial oil field to go into production in Alaska. Six years later it had discovered the second biggest field in Alaska, at Cook Inlet. The success of the Richfield company was due to its chairman, Charlie Jones, famous throughout the American oil industry, a giant of a man, six feet seven and broad-shouldered in proportion, dominating, outspoken, extroverted and colorful. He was the kind of oilman about whom Bob's father used to speak with relish when he got back home from a trip to Texas, the kind of character who had caught Bob's imagination and awakened his interest in the oil industry. Bob knew a lot about Charlie Jones and liked what he knew. Charlie had done business with Bob's father and respected Hugo greatly. When as a result of his acquisition of Wilshire Bob made visits to Los Angeles, he had met Charlie. In 1965 Charlie was thinking of retiring. It was very much on his mind that there was no crown prince to run his beloved Richfield after he left it.

Looking around for some company with which Atlantic might be merged to solve the problem of its lack of crude, Bob's eye alighted on Richfield. He was well aware that three years previously the U.S. Department of Justice had filed an action against the Richfield Oil Corporation alleging violation of the Federal antitrust laws. The charge against Richfield was that twenty-six years previously, in 1936, the company had violated the antitrust laws when it merged with two other companies, the Sinclair Oil Corporation and the Cities Service Company. The alleged illegality consisted in the fact that Richfield did not compete territorially with the other two, and therefore had acquired an unfair advantage over its competitors, an advantage of a kind which the antitrust laws had been enacted to prohibit. The decision of the Department of Justice to prosecute Richfield for a merger which had taken place 26 years previously, and been approved at the time by the courts in California, created much controversy. Since nobody had questioned the legality of the 1936 transaction until 1962, a year after John F. Kennedy had been inaugurated, many people attributed this initiative on the part of the government to the new President's hostility toward the leaders of the oil industry. "Kennedy," it was said, "is out to get the oil barons."

Various opinions were expressed about the move made by the Department of Justice, but none so vigorously as that of Charlie Jones. A man whose wrath it had never been hard to arouse, he now fired every gun he had, accompanying his broadside with a declaration that he would appeal the department's ruling, fight the suit to the death and win. As the weeks went by and the lawyers on both sides did their work, Charlie Jones became less confident that he was going to win his case. He began to ponder whether it would be better to accept the department's demand that Richfield sever its relationship with Sinclair and Cities Service, either by liquidating Richfield altogether or by merging with another company which would not be in a monopolistic situation. The department had obligingly supplied him with a list of companies that they would find acceptable.

Though the greatest secrecy was enjoined upon all parties, rumors of a new merger were rife. Charlie Jones's telephone was busy with callers making offers from oil firms, some of which were on the department's list and others not. The rumors sent up the value of Richfield shares substantially. The chairman of Sinclair hoped that he might become the new owner of Richfield and worked hard to bring this about. His ardor was matched by the chairman of Cities Service, who had the same idea. But Charlie Jones was not of such a mind. If there was to be a new boss of Richfield, he wanted him to be a man after his own heart. And he had made up his mind that, provided the terms were acceptable, that man would be Robert Anderson.

Bob did not know at the time that Charlie Jones had gone a long way down the road to making him his heir, but he knew all about the action which the Department of Justice had initiated against Richfield, and he knew Charlie Jones's hopes of winning his appeal were on the wane. He knew, too, that his own company, Atlantic, was on the Department of Justice's list of eligibles. Bob was acquainted with the chairman of one of the three companies involved in the suit, Cities Service's Burl Watson, as both were members of the National Petroleum Council. Bob had asked Watson to have lunch with him in New York. They had a frank discussion about Richfield's—and Charlie Jones's—predicament. At the end of the lunch Watson telephoned Charlie Jones in Los Angeles. "Charlie," he said, "I've got a friend of yours right here with me. We've been talking. I think he ought to come out there and talk to *you*." He handed the telephone to Bob. Charlie Jones said, "Bob, why don't you come out here and have lunch?"

Bob flew out to Los Angeles at once. In spite of the rapport between the two men and the interest they had in making a deal, their first meeting did not bear fruit. Charlie Jones wanted a cash deal, at $80 per Richfield share; Anderson wanted a stock deal and said that $80 a share was too high. A few weeks later they met again; this second meeting also produced no result. During September Richfield's stock continued to appreciate. Several companies made offers to Jones, which he declined. Then, as he recorded in his memoirs:

A curious event occurred. One of our Washington lawyers called to tell me that a Mr. Cladouhos, an Anti-Trust Division lawyer assigned to the case, had suggested that Richfield settle the suit by merging with Atlantic Refining Company. The Division had earlier suggested a merger, but this was the first time it had named a partner. The suggestion seemed unusual, but I concluded that Bob Anderson's lawyers had probably been exploring the Justice Department's attitude towards a merger with Richfield and had thus given Cladouhos this particular inspiration.

More offers for Richfield followed. The approach made by Burl Watson, chairman of Cities Service, which already owned about 30 percent of Richfield, was extremely attractive. Bob Anderson had balked when Charlie Jones had asked for $80 a share; Watson did not demur when Jones told him that he would have to pay *at least* $80 a share. Jones told Watson that he would leave Los Angeles the following day and meet him in New York. "Within an hour," Jones recorded in his memoirs, "Bob telephoned from Philadelphia—he must have been prescient, because his timing was perfect. A day later, and there would probably have been no merger of Atlantic and Richfield." Charlie Jones's account of what happened from then on is as follows:

Bob began the conversation with the usual trading talk: "Price too high," and so on.
"I think you should just forget the matter," I said.
"Well," he responded, "I'd like to talk to you, and I'll come to Los Angeles."
"Sorry, but I'm leaving tomorrow morning for New York."
This did not deter Bob, and I agreed to see him at my hotel on my arrival in New York the next evening, September 15.

When the two men had had their last meeting, at Jones's ranch in Idaho, Charlie had shown Bob the draft of a merger agreement which he had prepared. Charlie was proud of his draft: "It was a succinct piece of craftsmanship." But it was incomplete in that one detail had been omitted: *the terms.* When Bob met Charlie in New York he handed him his own proposal for a merger. Bob's proposal was word for word what Charlie had shown him back in Idaho, except for the terms which had now been added. These were Bob's. Charlie Jones recorded:

> As I studied the proposal, I realized that he was making a sincere try for an agreement. Putting the offer in the context of the [draft] which I had given him was a superb bit of psychology on Bob's part.
>
> In sum, the offer was to give Richfield's stockholders one share of a new $3 Atlantic convertible preference stock for each share of Richfield. Each share of the preference would be convertible into $85/100$ of a share of Atlantic common stock. Of course, the value of the offer would have to be judged by a financial expert, but my own judgment was that the security would sell in the marketplace for $80.
>
> "Bob," I said, "you might have yourself a deal."

The merger now required ratification by the two boards, Atlantic Refining and Richfield. It was then necessary to obtain the approval of the shareholders, the permission of the Department of Justice, the resolution of the antitrust suit—at this stage a formality since the department had helped bring about the merger—and, finally, an agreement with the Internal Revenue Service that the merger would be tax-free to Richfield's stockholders.

All these conditions were met in the next three months, but in the middle of December, only two weeks before the meeting with the Richfield stockholders, there was a crisis. When the Department of Justice had agreed to the merger, and had dismissed the antitrust suit, it had made some stipulations which at the time had seemed innocuous, and in the view of the department they certainly were. The Internal Revenue Service, not at all interested in the merger but very interested in the application of the tax laws, now announced that these stipulations would require the stockholders to pay a tax on the transaction. This news was bad: paying such a tax would make the deal much less attractive to the stockholders, and a majority of them, therefore, would almost certainly vote against the merger at the coming meeting. In that case the whole deal would have to go back to the drawing board. Once there it might never come to the table again, or, at any rate, not come back to the same table. At best there would be a period of doubt which would bring down the price of Richfield's stock. A cloud now obscured the Jones-Anderson sun.

To meet this unforeseen last-minute threat to his hopes, Charlie Jones went to Washington, temporarily closing his house in Los Angeles and living in a hotel. From there he sallied forth daily for discussions with officials of the Internal Revenue Service and with anybody else he thought could help him. Because the deadline for the stockholders' meeting was only a few days ahead, the temperature in which Charlie's activities were conducted was high. Two days before the deadline the Internal Revenue Service was still silent. Then, in a flash as it seemed at the time, the IRS lawyers announced their agreement. When the stockholders of Richfield met at noon, December 30, 1965, as his last official act as chairman of the company, Charlie Jones was able to ask them to approve the merger with Atlantic.

CHAPTER FIVE

In the merger of Atlantic and Richfield, Bob achieved a long-standing ambition. He had always believed that not only the future of the oil industry, but that of the United States, lay in the Western states and in the Pacific. The merger had oriented Atlantic on the East Coast to the West in a big way. Bob has long been an outspoken proponent of what he calls the westernization of the world. "The next century," he says, "will be the century of the Pacific Basin." On a more personal level, the merger gratified him because the Richfield acquisition "filled in" his interests from his old base, his beloved Rockies, to the shores of the Pacific.

However, the merger had also created a number of practical problems. The immediate one in January 1966, after the marriage had been legally consummated, was how to bring them together in a structure and with a policy which would bring out the best in both companies, separated physically by several thousand miles of territory and psychologically by different ideas of how a successful oil-producing company should be run.

At the outset there was trouble. Though Bob had issued instructions that the unification of the two companies was to be conducted on the principle of "the best people in the best jobs," some of Richfield's top executives soon began to complain that Atlantic was being treated as though it had the lion's share of the "best people." Edward M. (Mo) Benson, Richfield's forty-five-year-old general manager of production operations, felt this so strongly that in the middle of January he wrote to Charlie Jones and told him so, attaching an organization chart to prove his point and concluding: "I thought you should be aware that the only name listed from your company's production department is a man who is already past retirement age." Mo's letter made a deep and instant impression on Jones, who immediately telephoned him and asked him to have fifty or so of his production and exploration executives in the boardroom for a working lunch the following Monday. This was done. Charlie placed Mo next to the one and only guest, Bob Anderson. Their conversation had three results: there was a reallocation of responsibilities in the new company which gave several important production and exploration posts to Richfield men, among them a vice presidency to Mo; secondly, Bob renamed the new company to include the name "Richfield" so as to preserve and raise the morale of Richfield employees discomfited by being taken over by a rival (the company officially became the Atlantic Richfield Company, or ARCO, in May 1966); thirdly, Bob established his hopes for oil in Alaska. Mo Benson recorded a few years later: "After we had talked about the men in Richfield who could make a contribution to exploration and production, I told Bob I was leaving on 17 February to fly to the North Slope. He said, 'Would it be all right if I go along with you?' So, being a bright employee, I said that I would let the chairman come along."

They went up to the Prudhoe field. The Richfield men on the slope met Bob for the first time. One of the drilling foremen, Benny Laudermilk, recalls that "Mr. Anderson shook hands with all of us roughnecks. He carried an old paper sack, and in it were a pair of cowboy boots and Levi's that looked like they should have been thrown away. . . . He took his suit off and put on the old Levi's and the boots and said, 'Let's go.' "

At this time Bob believed that a big field might be opened up in Alaska. "Bob Anderson," Mo Benson recorded ten years later, "has got this extra sense. He sensed that Alaska was going to be something very big."

On the whole, the two partners to the merger settled down with each other extremely well. They had been run very differently. Though the administration of Atlantic had changed since Bob had become chief executive, it continued to be a relaxed, quiet, well-mannered kind of company, an operation run by gentlemen in a gentlemanly kind of way. After Bob took over, Atlantic had given up a centralized organization within which total information was exchanged only at the top and replaced it with a system of relatively self-directing separate groups, each virtually an independent company, with its own district in which to operate, its own geologists, engineers and drilling experts. Richfield, on the other hand, had been run by Charlie Jones. "If Charlie Jones did not do something," said Mo Benson, "nobody did. He was the Great White Father."

Because of the decentralization and autonomy, the atmosphere within Atlantic was comfortable. Inside Richfield, where so much depended on the mood and will of one strong, volatile, often explosive individual, who relied on instinct and hunch and did not work through a stable and rationalized hierarchy, the atmosphere was often tense. There were jealousies, suspicions and rivalries. Since Charlie had kept everybody in the dark about his intentions in the weeks before the deal these tensions had multiplied, and when the nature of the merger had been revealed, apprehension and distraction, compounded by senior men's fears for their future, were at their height.

At the time of the merger, depressed and apprehensive Richfield executives were saying to their friends, "Atlantic men are going to treat Richfield men like mushrooms: keep us in the dark, cover us up with manure and then can us." After a few days under Anderson's leadership the story changed somewhat: "Now we don't know who the mushrooms are." Richfield men continued to be apprehensive because control of their key operations in production and exploration would be in Dallas, not Los Angeles, but gradually their anxieties decreased. Bob Wycoff, then a Richfield man, now president of ARCO, recalled the process by which trust and confidence developed. In the early days Louis Davis, an expert oilman later to become a member of the ARCO board, and a few Atlantic colleagues came to Los Angeles from Dallas for a two-day conference. Wycoff was deeply impressed by them and by their attitude toward their Richfield counterparts. "These people had come all this way to tour our operations, not to tell us what should be done, but to listen to our advice. They didn't want to listen to our top managers; they wanted to hear from *each* geologist, *each* engineer, *each* production manager. They listened, they asked questions, they showed they respected everybody. After the two-day conference was over one of our engineers said, 'We've been given more management direction in the last two days than we've had in the last ten years.' " From then, the mushroom metaphor was no longer heard.

The object of the merger between Atlantic and Richfield was not merger for merger's sake, or to have a bigger operation, but to solve Atlantic's central problem—obtaining more crude oil. "Crude production has always been the absolute heart of the industry," Bob Anderson had said at the time. But the merger had not solved the problem. Bob had moved in on Richfield because Richfield had leases in Alaska and Atlantic had not: Atlantic had tried to get some but had failed, outbid by Richfield and its Alaska partner, the Humble Oil Refining Company of Houston, Texas. He had great faith in those leases, as did Louis Davis, then head of Atlantic's North American Producing Division. When Bob asked Louis what he thought about a prospective merger, Davis recorded, "I said that it was the most wonderful thing we could do because we would acquire all of that Alaska acreage owned by Richfield and Humble."

Their optimism about Alaska was not generally shared in Atlantic, and by no means universally in Richfield. In any case, the day when the discovery would be made was some years in the future. In January 1966 the new company was still short of crude. In fact, ARCO's position had worsened, since Richfield had been even shorter of crude than Atlantic. In the first months, therefore, the emphasis was on increasing the new company's supply of crude. It was urgent. The fact that the activities of the two companies were separated by the Rockies was a help: Atlantic could continue to operate in the East and Richfield in the West. But Atlantic's production and exploration men, operating from Dallas, were on the whole more widely experienced than the Californians, and Bob introduced Dallas expertise steadily into the development of Richfield's resources. In this he was helped by Dow Hamm's enthusiasm. The old Dallas entrepreneur had also been rooting for the merger, urging it on his colleagues in Dallas. "Richfield had a lot of undeveloped properties," he recorded later. "They had a lot of production in California. We knew how to make it produce more than they had been producing from it." Dow Hamm told his Dallas expansionists: "If you ever want a market on the West Coast this is your last chance of a real deal . . . this is your last call to dinner, boys." They took their chance. Bob's difficulty was not only to ensure that Atlantic's men did not appear to be crowding their Richfield opposite numbers, but also that within the Atlantic host the young Turks from Dallas did not seem to be preferred to their brethren back in Philadelphia. In his post-merger reorganization Bob had to be a diplomat as well as a boss.

The reorganization and the release of talent did something to produce more crude. At the time of the merger, production of the combined companies was running at 188,200 barrels a day, against a refining output of 373,900 barrels a day. This was below a fifty percent "sufficiency ratio." On becoming executive chairman of Atlantic, Bob had immediately upped the companies exploration and development budgets. In 1965 geophysical expenditure was 71 percent higher than the previous year and 45 percent over planned outlays. Bob now did the same thing for ARCO. In early 1966 the word went out: "More crude from American sources." The offensive was to be led by Louis Davis, but to be launched in California. It consisted of plans for 70 new onshore and 180 offshore wells. Though ARCO was to work old Richfield territories, the methods were to be Atlantic's. Richfield was required to disband some of its own drilling rigs and roustabout crews and contract out to specialist drilling companies that worked more effectively and at less cost. ARCO also adapted Atlantic's use of such new techniques as water flooding to improve pressures and flue gas injection to flush out more oil from the natural reservoir. By the end of the year, crude reserves had gone up by nearly 30 percent, and Louis Davis could report that by 1975 ARCO would be able to produce twice as much crude as it was then producing.

There now loomed the question of how far the existing oil supplies of the United States could meet rapidly increasing demands on them for the future. Early in 1968 Bill Kieschnick was transferred from the Central Region to become head of a new activity, Synthetic Crude Operations—the breaking of new ground in the development of coal, shale and tar sands in the search for alternative energy sources. As it turned out two things were to happen in 1968 which made ARCO's share of these problems in a sense academic: the discovery of the vast field on the North Slope of Alaska, and the merger with Sinclair.

Sinclair Oil, headquartered in New York, was the creation of one man, as colorful an individual as the oil industry had ever seen. Harry Sinclair, born in 1876, was the son of a small drugstore owner in Independence, Kansas. As a boy, outside school hours, he operated a laundry and a cylinder gramophone at local fairs, and raised chickens. When his father died, he took over the drugstore, hired a pharmacist and took a course in pharmacy himself. Oil was booming in Kansas in the early 1900s and Harry, a natural gambler, invested the drugstore takings in it, losing the lot and the store as well. He was penniless and unemployed. Then an incident occurred of which the account vouchsafed by Harry Sinclair was never universally accepted. He claimed that in the course of cleaning a shotgun he accidentally blew the top off his big toe. This left him crippled for life, but with the substantial insurance payment from which he benefited he was able to buy himself back into oil, beginning by providing timber for the building of derricks. By the time he was thirty he had made himself a fortune out of oil.

In 1923 came the Teapot Dome scandal: the control of leases of oil fields in Wyoming, previously reserved for the U.S. Navy, was removed from the Navy Department to the Department of the Interior, which subsequently leased the field to private oil buyers. The scandal arose when it was revealed that the secretary of the interior, Albert Fall, had suddenly added large tracts of land to his ranch, with, it was alleged, money provided by one of the new owners of the Teapot Dome leases, Harry Sinclair. After much lengthy litigation the leases were canceled in 1927, and Fall spent a year in jail. For contempt of the Senate, Sinclair also was sent to jail in Washington for six months. By one means or another he got himself classified as an invalid. It was said that his Rolls-Royce collected him every morning and took him out for "treatment," returning him every night with a hot-water bottle filled with Scotch. One story relates that he did not go to jail at all because a well-paid stand-in served his time. Sinclair Oil continued to expand. Harry had leases in many foreign parts, including Russia, and entered into two interesting ventures with British Petroleum: one to take Middle East oil from them to sell in the United States; the other in 1952, when British Petroleum had to leave Iran, to introduce the British company to the North Slope explorations in Alaska, securing rights to thousands of acres. Harry died of cancer in 1956, a gambler to the last, having made Sinclair the eighth largest oil company in the United States. In the early 1960s, Sinclair and British Petroleum drilled extensively in Alaska, but by 1965 they had decided to terminate their operations completely, although they held on to their leases.

In October 1968 the conglomerate of Gulf & Western, headed by Austrian-born Charles G. Bludhorn, decided to try to take over Sinclair. Previously nobody seems to have thought of merging with Sinclair, apart from Robert O. Anderson. What had gotten *him* around to the thought—he was also wondering about the possibility of merging with companies other than Sinclair—was ARCO's recent discovery of a huge oil field at Prudhoe Bay on the North Slope. This news meant that ARCO's crude-refining ratio had been stood on its head. ARCO, which a few months earlier had been looking for crude to supply its refining plant, would now have to look for refining plants—and sales outlets—to match up with its production of crude. ARCO's headquarters were now in New York. Bob had moved them there from Philadelphia a few months previously because he had concluded that the top management of ARCO should live and work in a much more competitive atmosphere than Philadelphia was able to provide. The move was naturally not popular with the top managers, who had lived in Philadelphia for years. Bob read in his evening newspaper one Friday night that Sinclair was in danger of being taken over, and that its chairman, Pendleton Thomas, was going to resist this. The newspaper also made it clear that now that Gulf & Western

THE WILDCATTER : 71

was making a move, several other companies were ready to bid for Sinclair.

Bob was planning to fly west that night and to go off with Barbara on Saturday morning for a week's horseback riding in the New Mexico mountains. He telephoned Pen Thomas. They met that night. Bob recounts: "I said I'd just heard the news, and I didn't know if a meeting would serve any purpose, but if he had any interest I'd like to get together with him. At this time we saw this as filling the gap between the East and West coasts. Pen Thomas did not want to be taken over by this vast conglomerate headed by a man whom he did not particularly admire, offering terms Thomas told him bluntly were 'Chinese paper.' Pen Thomas knew ARCO was a likable outfit—at any rate he had nothing against us. Our assets dovetailed."

ARCO now had vast supplies of crude—Alaska had done that for it—and Sinclair had big refining operations and thousands of service stations, plus vast amounts of leases in the Prudhoe Bay area. ARCO was strong in retailing on the East Coast and strong on the West Coast; most of Sinclair's pumps were in the Midwest. There would be coast-to-coast coverage. The only snag could be that the Department of Justice would judge the coverage to be so good as to prevent competition. Pen Thomas pointed this out. "In that case," said Bob, "we shall offer to sell all assets which the law holds to stand in the way of a fair deal." (The Department of Justice did raise an objection, so ARCO and Sinclair sold the requisite number of assets—many of them to British Petroleum—to obtain permission for the merger.)

The two men shook hands. Bob then surprised Pen Thomas, as in similar circumstances he has surprised so many of his acquaintances before and since, by mentioning that, his proposal having been made, he would fly to New Mexico that night and spend a week on the ranch. "But Brad will be around if you want to pursue the matter." Pen Thomas telephoned Bradshaw the following Monday morning. He had discussed the matter with key members of his board and top executives and now had a number of requests. If these were acceptable to Bob Anderson, he was sure the deal could be recommended by the Sinclair board. But the matter had to be settled by a board meeting to be held three days later, otherwise there would be a delay, in which case it was highly probable that Gulf & Western would be able to mobilize enough support to enable them to take over. Bradshaw was shaken by the speed with which events had moved. He had been warned by Bob that he might be telephoned for further "talk" and more information, but he had assumed that Bob had not expected to have to make such a fundamental decision in such haste. Bradshaw met Thomas that night. The following day they met again and drew up a one-page summary of terms for a merger for submission to Sinclair's board the following Thursday. Brad tried to get in touch with Bob several times and failed. While he was wondering what to do, the telephone rang. It was Bob Anderson. Riding through a village on the edge of the New Mexican desert, Bob had gotten off his horse and walked over to a pay phone. Bradshaw heard the words: "Hi, Brad. Anything happening?" Bradshaw outlined Pen Thomas's requirements. Bradshaw recorded for the archives: "Bob has a fast mind. As soon as I gave him the exchange ratios and the convertibility of the preference stock, and he knew precisely what we were paying, he said, 'Well, I guess that's all right.' If he had said anything else, it would have been very, very difficult." Pen Thomas put his recommendation to his board, which approved it. The merger of Sinclair with ARCO—technically, Sinclair became part of ARCO— became official and legal on March 4, 1969. It was the largest merger made in the United States up to that time.

As had been the case only three years previously, there was now again the problem of merging two large staffs. There had been an overlap between Atlantic and Richfield, but it was nothing compared to the overlap between ARCO and Sinclair. The problem was not so much of retailers as of production personnel. Both ARCO and Sinclair had well-established production bases in the Midwest and Southwest, the two headquarters being Dallas, Texas (ARCO), and Tulsa, Oklahoma (Sinclair). It was not just a case of some of the Sinclair production staff doing what ARCO people could do; there had been a great deal of overstaffing at Sinclair, cases of two people to do one man's job. Mo Benson recorded that "Sinclair's organization was weaker in virtually all aspects than were either Atlantic's or Richfield's." Louis Davis said, "Sinclair had a much poorer grade of people. They were poorly run and poorly staffed . . . they didn't pay well, they didn't treat their people well." Not many of the top Sinclair men were brought into the top echelon of ARCO. Many Sinclair men lower down the hierarchy were pensioned off on the good terms requested by Pen Thomas and agreed to by ARCO before Thomas put his recommendation of the deal before his directors. But so that there should be no feeling on the part of Sinclair executives that they were being arbitrarily pushed out by ARCO men, a consulting firm was called in to discuss redundancies with Mo Benson for ARCO and Daniel Almen for Sinclair.

The merger worked out well. It was effected by a remarkable piece of timing and judgment on Bob Anderson's part. Many of the executives and shareholders of Sinclair believed at the time, and continue to believe, that Sinclair could have ridden out the threat of a takeover, that Pen Thomas "panicked." But if Pen Thomas had turned down the generous terms Bob agreed to, which he clearly understood were good for the moment but would not be repeated, and *then* had had to give in to Gulf & Western, or anybody else, he and his colleagues would have been deeply mortified. Bob Anderson seized his moment, gave Thomas an offer which, indeed, he could not refuse; he also solved his crude-refining problem and lifted ARCO into seventh position among the great oil companies of America.

At about this time, shortly before the Prudhoe Bay discovery and the merger with Sinclair, Bob Anderson was considering another acquisition. He was still concerned about his central problem of getting more crude and was anxious to carry out his six-point program for ARCO's future—in particular, securing the acquisition of other valuable sources of oil, especially oil shale. He had made inquiries about the Anaconda Company, which was well equipped, with the expertise to mine oil shale on a large scale, and he thought an acquisition would suit both companies. He and Bradshaw had meetings with the top Anaconda men in late 1968 and early 1969.

The venture which later became Anaconda first saw the light of day on October 1875 when a veteran of the Civil War, Michael Hickey, made a little hole on a hill overlooking what is now Butte City, Montana, and staked out a quartz claim. Thinking about what to call his little "mine," he remembered reading during the war about the Army of the North enveloping the Army of the South "like an anaconda." He called his mine "Anaconda." In 1882, Marcus Daly, a penniless Irish immigrant who had been a dock laborer in New York, came to Butte City in search of gold and silver. He was soon in charge of the Anaconda mine, but within ten years it was not gold, silver or quartz, but copper that was making a fortune for him. When Thomas Edison, the inventor of the electric bulb, opened the Pearl Street (New York) generating station to supply the streets of New York City with electric light, a great demand for copper wire was at once created. By 1890 Daly was operating the largest single copper enterprise in the world. In the early 1900s Anaconda began to mine in Mexico. Later it also operated large interests in South America, notably in Peru. But by the time ARCO began to take an interest in Anaconda, the company's most important outpost was in Chile, and the Chilean economy was primarily dependent on the export of copper. In 1929 it was the eighth largest company listed on the New York Stock Exchange.

By the mid-sixties, Anaconda was encountering critical problems in Chile. Nationalist feeling demanded government involvement in, or control of, the copper mines. In an attempt to forestall out-and-out nationalization—"Chileanization"—of their two most valuable possessions, the Chuquicamata and El Salvador mines, Anaconda agreed to form a joint company with the Chilean government's copper corporation.

At this time Anderson and Bradshaw approached Anaconda about a merger. The Anaconda directors were sufficiently interested to get their lawyers to work on the possibility. But eventually their board declined to go forward, partly because they did not relish going under the wing of ARCO, the larger company of the two, and partly because political conditions in Chile were becoming so delicate that any major move on Anaconda's part outside Chile might lead to complications inside that country. So in a friendly way, ARCO and Anaconda tapered off their talks about doing business together. It was a lucky day for Bob. The discovery of the Prudhoe Bay field was only a few months ahead. If the merger had taken place first, Anaconda would have been entitled to a huge portion of the rise in the price of ARCO's stock occasioned by the Prudhoe Bay discovery. In addition, ARCO would have had to help bear the damage done to Anaconda in 1970 when its prize possession, the Chuquicamata mine, was nationalized outright by the newly established regime of President Salvador Allende Gossens with no compensation. As a result, Anaconda lost three quarters of its earnings and two thirds of its tonnage—the second largest corporate loss in a single year in the history of American business.

In 1973 the short-lived Allende regime was overthrown by a military coup, as a result of which Anaconda later obtained considerable redress in the form of a commitment of payment for its assets over a period of several years. But this did not offer a great prospect, and Anaconda's activities on American soil did not hold out great promise. The company looked vulnerable, and the severe American recession of 1974–75, which caused a critical drop in demand for copper, put it into extreme difficulty. "Once we lost Chile, I knew Anaconda was on the block," said William Quigley, who had served as vice-chairman of the company through all its vicissitudes. "I knew we were ripe for something." Anaconda was. Takeover attempts began in the second half of 1975. Coincidentally, Bob had come to the conclusion that the time had come for ARCO to acquire substantial mining skills in order to exploit its extensive shale oil holdings. Part of the development scheme which ARCO contemplated was a plan to open the largest underground mine in the world, which would be three times as large as the biggest mining ever undertaken. The cost of mining was so high that an investment of between $2 and $3 billion would be required. Bob knew what had to be done, but had deep misgivings about ARCO undertaking an operation of this magnitude without having substantial in-house capability and experience. Anaconda had it. For ARCO to acquire Anaconda seemed desirable.

The merger was agreed upon by the two companies in July 1976. In October the Federal Trade Commission formally blocked the merger, claiming that it would lessen competition in the sale of uranium oxide. The courts did not hold for the FTC and blessed the merger, which was finally executed in January 1977. Anaconda, more than a hundred years old, became an operating subsidiary of ARCO.

The acquisition of Anaconda and the oil shale mining it enabled

ARCO to embark on did not pay off, however. The Anaconda venture was a casualty of the overly strong dollar which dominated the economic scene from 1979. As a result of the virtual doubling of the value of the dollar vis-à-vis other international currencies, virtually all mining operations in the United States became unprofitable. With the combined pressures of high labor cost and environmental requirements, and declining prices for dollar producers, the bulk of the mining industry was extinguished. Anaconda was no exception, and in 1985 most of its operations were terminated. Only the coal operations remain today, and ARCO constitutes one of the largest coal-producing companies in the United States. Economic pressures have pushed the coal company into the world market, currently with operations in Australia, and new ventures in Indonesia and the People's Republic of China. "Anaconda," says Bob today, "was purely and simply a casualty of what the United States government allowed to happen to the dollar, of the enormous increase in our national trade deficit, another casualty of the deindustrialization of America which has characterized the 1980s. My consolation is that if we had not bought Anaconda, and had gone ahead with our own vast mining investment, the damage done to ARCO would have been much greater."

CHAPTER SIX

Bob Anderson, in his lifelong pursuit of crude oil—"the absolute heart of the industry"—had believed for many years that there was big oil in Alaska. Long before he had acquired leases of his own on the North Slope by the merger of Hondo with Atlantic Refining, he had been studying what various oil companies were doing on and around the Arctic Circle; in particular, he had kept an observant eye on the activities of Richfield in that part of the world. "But even if there *is* oil there," a cautious colleague asked him, "how the hell will you get it out?" "Through a pipeline," said Bob, who had been building pipelines since he was twenty.

In 1964, with his encouragement, Bill Kieschnick, who was in charge of Atlantic's Alaska operations, had signed up Lee Wilson to go to Alaska and drill. Wilson had been born into drilling wells. He had seen his first well "shot" when he was four years old in the days when a well was started by lowering a charge of nitroglycerine to the bottom of the hole and detonating it, the explosion causing the oil to gush. In the spring of 1965, Lee Wilson drilled four wells. They were dry. Wilson moved his rig to Cook Inlet, where Richfield was also drilling. Then came the merger.

To see Alaska as Bob Anderson saw it at the time of the merger, and as he saw it again a year later when he had to pronounce the sensational "yes" or "no" which would either leave ARCO as just another oil company or make it the owner of the world's greatest proven oil field, we must go back to the middle fifties. In 1956 Richfield was concerned about the high purchasing cost of crude oil. Somehow, somewhere, Richfield had to find much cheaper crude. Long before this Richfield had looked around in Alaska, and in 1939 had made some small exploration on the west side of Cook Inlet, the long bay on the southern coast of Alaska that runs up to Anchorage. The Second World War interrupted exploration in that area, and Richfield's next operation began in 1956, about forty miles southwest of Anchorage on the Kenai Peninsula. The following year Richfield's initiative was rewarded by the discovery of the Swanson River field, the first commercial oil field in Alaska. The first well was drilled.

There now came a temporary setback, soon dealt with, but, though it was not realized at the time, one which looked bad for the future. A number of American conservationist organizations in the "lower forty-eight" (the Alaskan's term for the rest of the United States) complained that the new oil field would endanger the moose on the Kenai Moose Range. A meeting of oilmen with prominent environmentalists was arranged by the secretary of the interior, Fred Seaton. This meeting proved amicable and constructive. Richfield was allowed to proceed. But five years later there was another protest from conservationists and the United States Court of Appeals supported them, declaring most leases held in Alaska null and void. By now millions of dollars had been invested in Alaska. Richfield and its colleagues contested the court's ruling. Two years later, in 1965, the United States Supreme Court decided the issue in favor of the companies, and the way was open to the development of the Alaskan oil industry. By now Richfield had made an important discovery offshore in Cook Inlet, the second biggest find in Alaska. By now, too, the new state of Alaska—the forty-ninth, established in 1959—whose development had been accelerated by Richfield's discovery on the Kenai Peninsula in 1957, was enjoying large bonuses, rentals and tax revenues from the oil companies, as well as benefiting from the large capital investment made by the companies, outlays which were increasing every year.

By the time Bob had his eye on Richfield it was clear to him, as it was to Charlie Jones, that while the fields in Cook Inlet and on the Kenai Peninsula were not to be overlooked, the potential eight hundred miles to the north, where the land sloped down from Brooks Range northward to the Arctic Sea, was immense. This vast basin was rich in deposits of marine sediments. Some locations on this North Slope had been reserved by the U.S. government for the Navy. Richfield had drilled some of those for the government, and consequently knew oil and gas were in them. They knew, too, from surface geology and seismic work that there were large structures of the kind in which large deposits of oil might well be found. The North Slope, however, was remote. It could not be reached by land across the Brooks Range. It was possible to fly over the mountains; otherwise the region was accessible only by sea, for a few weeks in the year, on the north coast at Point Barrow. An exploration program would involve opening an overland supply route where the Alaska Railroad ended, roughly halfway between the north and south coasts of Alaska, using the Anaktuvuk Pass through Brooks Range to the Arctic Slope going down to the sea.

In 1964 Richfield owned nearly a million acres on the North Slope. But that year the Alaskan State Government offered, among other sites, a large tract at Prudhoe Bay, on the north coast, two hundred miles east of Point Barrow. Charlie Jones was convinced that this tract had oil. One thing was clear: if it did, a huge pipeline would have to be built to get the oil out. The cost of doing so would be vast, so only if there were an immense amount of oil in the bay would the venture prove profitable. Enormous sums would be required for ships and shore facilities. Sinclair and British Petroleum had drilled for two years on the North Slope and had found six dry holes. It was all a large and costly risk. To lessen it, Charlie Jones offered a partnership in the venture to SOCAL, the Standard Oil Company of California. Much to his disappointment, they turned it down. He then asked Humble Oil to go in with him. They agreed. With that backing Charlie secured as much of the North Slope land as he could afford. British Petroleum secured most of the rest.

At the time of the Atlantic Richfield merger in January 1966,

Richfield had three thousand tons of drilling equipment in Fairbanks, ready to move north. A four-engine turboprop Hercules C-130 air-freighter had been chartered from Lockheed to fly the equipment to the North Slope. The uncertainties immediately after the merger delayed the decision to move. Dow Hamm and the Atlantic exploration men, while enthusiastic about the North Slope, were dubious about the particular location favored by Richfield. The Richfield men, on the other hand, wanted to go ahead with the plans they had made before the merger and did not care whether the Atlantic men agreed with them or not. In the interests of meeting expiration dates, Bob gave the Atlantic men the nod. The following month, Mo Benson, no longer general manager of operations for Richfield but vice president in charge of explorations, engineering and production for ARCO, was able to start moving equipment, and drilling began at a location inland, sixty miles south of Prudhoe Bay, on an Atlantic wildcat called Suzie I. After ten months of drilling—they drilled to 11,000 feet—Suzie proved to be a dry hole. The well was plugged and abandoned in January 1967. There was disappointment. Charlie Jones, now a sick man, was downcast. But, as his colleagues told him, "We still have Prudhoe Bay." ARCO owned its tracts at Prudhoe Bay as a result of the original Richfield holdings acquired in the merger. In January 1967, just at the time when preparations were being made to plug and abandon Suzie I, the state of Alaska had put up seven more tracts for sale, including acreage offshore in Prudhoe Bay. Anderson, still convinced that there was big oil in Alaska, and that it could be at Prudhoe Bay, bought.

ARCO did "still have Prudhoe Bay," but having added another dry hole to the six which Sinclair and British Petroleum had left behind them on the slope, was it worth having another go? Mo Benson, feeling that Richfield must have the chance to reap the fruit of all the work the company had put in on the slope, and keen to prove himself in his new job, was all in favor. So was Louis Davis, now his boss, late of Atlantic. Davis had felt for years that in Dallas, Atlantic had as good an exploration and engineering team as any in the world, but that until Bob Anderson took over as chief executive the Atlantic men had never been given the chance to show their strength. Of Dow

Hamm, Lou's old boss in Atlantic, Mo Benson once said, "Dow once had the entire Persian Gulf tied up at one time, but when he took it to Philadelphia [the board] and asked them to let him go ahead, they laughed him out of the boardroom." Atlantic exploration and production men had acquired good sites and learned much know-how in Alaska: now, with Bob Anderson, a wildcatter himself, and a risk-taker, in charge, Atlantic would have its first great chance. There was pressure therefore from both the former companies to go on drilling in Alaska, although some in ARCO were for cutting their losses in Alaska and getting out.

There now followed a great debate within the company about what to do. Lee Wilson and his colleagues, including staff geologist Marvin D. Mangus, who, as a young man prospected the North Slope for the U.S. Geological Service twenty years previously, went to Dallas to present their case for continuing to drill. The matter was then taken to Philadelphia—still the headquarters of ARCO—where it was referred to the "Operating Officers Group." This, in effect, meant Robert O. Anderson. He had always believed in the North Slope. He saw that the venture in Prudhoe Bay would weld the two companies together as nothing else could. He gave the word to go ahead. "There was never any question that we would not go ahead and drill Prudhoe," he said afterwards. There was jubilation in ARCO, and also some muttering. The following month a cat (caterpillar) train began to plough through the snow to move the rig and the rest of the equipment from the site of Suzie I to Prudhoe Bay. At this time Charlie Jones was on his ranch in Idaho, suffering from an inflammation in his leg which was causing him considerable pain. He felt out of things; his morale was low. His body was in "the lower forty-eight," but his mind was in Alaska. Mo Benson recalled Bob saying to him, "Let Charlie know how things are going every day."

In the last week of April 1967 ARCO's team, led by Lee Wilson, began to drill a well, officially known as Prudhoe Bay State No. 1. It was the only well being drilled on the entire North Slope, "for all the rest had fled." The condition of permanent frost—permafrost—meant that during most of the next few months the work could not be continued. Drilling was resumed in October. First they struck shale, and they drilled through shale for a long time. But the shale showed oil, and the deeper they drilled the stronger were the "shows." About 7000 feet down in December, they found increasingly large amounts of natural gas. The drilling continued—the target depth was 13,000 feet—to 9000 feet and here came the oil. A great deal of oil, but bearing in mind where the oil was—nearly two miles under the sea, in the frozen recesses of distant Alaska—was there enough to make its extraction worthwhile?

When Bob heard the great news he got in touch with Lou Davis at once and talked to him at length. Lou was now head of ARCO's North American production. They agreed that a "confirmation" well must be started as soon as possible. The farther away the "confirmation" well was drilled, if it *did* confirm, the greater the size of the field would be revealed to be. But the farther away the second well was drilled, the greater the chance it would be dry. And when the second well had been drilled, perhaps there would be no oil, or little oil, in it, and the field, if field there were, would be proved to be a small one. If this turned out to be the case the whole Prudhoe Bay project would turn out to be an economic failure.

"How far away do you want to go for the second well?" asked Bob. Lou Davis said that according to the seismic charts he thought a seven-mile step-out to the south would prove the size of the field. "That's a hell of a long way," said Bob, "but let's go."

They drilled the second well—Sag River State No. 1—in midsummer 1968. This time, they really hit oil! There was to be absolute secrecy. The radio was not to be used: reports were to be flown down from the bay to Anchorage to be opened by John Sweet, the exploration manager, who sat behind a sealed glass panel. Lee Wilson, in Alaska as drilling superintendent, was sitting outside the panel and watched Sweet read the first log.

Sweet could not contain his jubilation and shouted "Wahoo!" at the top of his voice. "They heard it all over the building," recorded Wilson. "I thought, There goes our secrecy." The more they drilled, the more they hit. "We just kept drilling and coring, drilling and coring, and we got nothing but oil." Every now and then, Lou Davis said, "I'd call Bob and tell him we'd gotten another billion barrels.

That went on for weeks and weeks." Along the seven miles between Prudhoe Bay State No. 1 and Sag River State No. 1—at about 8000 feet—there was nothing but oil.

Influenced by the publicly expressed skepticism and envy evinced by some of the oil companies that had pulled out, the New York Stock Exchange recorded doubts as to whether there could be that much oil in Alaska. In order to ensure credibility, Bob called in the oil industry's outstanding consultants, De Golyer and MacNaughton, which, in a lengthy and learned letter to ARCO intended for publication, declared, "This important discovery could develop into a field with recoverable reserves of some 5 to 10 billion barrels of oil, which would rate as one of the largest petroleum accumulations known to the world today." Once he had read it, Bob ordered the immediate publication of the report. On its release, Atlantic Richfield's shares on the New York Stock Exchange soared. So did those of all companies known—or thought—to have leases around Prudhoe Bay. Corporations which a few hours previously had been skeptical about the value of ARCO's discoveries were now hailing them as if they had been their own. In London, British Petroleum, which after eight unproductive years had ceased all operations on the North Slope, now saw its shares rocket and helped their upward flight by reminding the world that they still retained their Alaskan leases.

A few weeks after the Prudhoe Bay discovery had been publicly announced, Bob Anderson and Mike Wright, the president of Humble, flew to London together to meet British Petroleum and discuss preliminary plans for the development of the field. Flying across the middle of the Atlantic, over dinner, Bob told Wright that when they met British Petroleum he would very much like to propose to them that ARCO and Humble buy British Petroleum out of Prudhoe Bay for $1 billion, which would be payable partly in cash, partly in crude oil. He pointed out to Mike that at that time the United Kingdom had serious balance of payments problems and that the British government, as a major owner in British Petroleum, could easily take the opportunity of making a quick profit on such a sale which could very much benefit their trade account. Furthermore, it would obviate the need for Britain to make a huge investment in

Alaska which would have to be made in a foreign currency. Unfortunately, this proposal, it was immediately clear, did not appeal to Wright; he thought the price Bob was suggesting was too high. He did not have Bob's faith in the potential of the Prudhoe field. Bob then seriously considered the possibility of ARCO's making the offer single-handedly, but on reflection reluctantly came to the conclusion that such a deal would be too much for ARCO to undertake on its own, particularly since Humble, as ARCO's partner in Prudhoe Bay, would have the right to back in on it later on any terms that suited it. So he dropped the idea. Looking back on it he said, "I think a billion dollars would have done it. I think BP would have accepted it. I think the British government would have been grateful." Events soon proved that Bob's proposal to Humble was sound.

The vast Prudhoe Bay oil field having been found, the next task was to provide the means of transporting the crude from the permanently frozen Arctic Ocean to a warm-water port equipped to handle it. Some consideration was given to using tankers to take it from Prudhoe Bay, or south through the Bering Strait to Anchorage, an idea favored initially by British Petroleum. Opinion was soon unanimous, however, that the only satisfactory method of transporting the oil was by way of a pipeline specially designed and constructed for that purpose. Several questions arose immediately: What should be its route? Where should the tanker port be located? How many pumping stations would be required to move the oil up and down across mountains and through the valleys for eight hundred miles to the sea? What kind of pipe was necessary to cope with the climatic conditions? For some hundreds of miles the pipe would have to run through, or above, the permafrost, some of it to a depth of 1500 feet below the surface. Parts of the pipeline would have to run through ground which in the spring would thaw, causing the pipe to shift in its moorings, become distorted and possibly break. What should be the caliber of the pipe? Of what metal should it be made? Who had the expertise to manufacture it? The most difficult question, because it was one which the oil industry had never before had to try to answer, was: What would be required to conduct oil, which would come from the well at a temperature of anything up to 160°F, through permafrost, of which the temperature would be many degrees below zero? To prevent the pipe, heated by the oil, from melting the surrounding permafrost, and consequently shifting dangerously in the ground, should the pipe be *refrigerated?* How much of the line should be carried above terra firma, say a foot above the ground as across the deserts of the Middle East, or maybe four feet, or more in some places? And how much should pass through the soil? How was the pipeline to be financed? To build and put it into position would cost about $900 million: where was that kind of money to come from? Finally, and, in the end, the most important two questions of all: What effects would the construction of the pipeline have on the Alaskan environment? And, to become of even more pressing concern, how would news of the construction of the pipeline affect the attitude of American environmentalists?

ARCO, its partner, Humble Oil, and British Petroleum made an announcement on February 10, 1969, which answered some of these questions. They said they had formed a company called the Trans-Alaska Pipeline System (TAPS) to plan, build and operate the pipeline. It would be a forty-eight-inch line, running eight hundred miles across Alaska from Prudhoe Bay in the north to some port on the southern coast; later it was announced that the port would be Valdez. Completion was expected three years later, in the early spring of 1972. Total cost was estimated at $900 million. Before the work on the pipeline could begin, it would be necessary to lay an all-weather supply road from Fairbanks, halfway up Alaska, where the highway terminated, up to Prudhoe Bay. To get equipment, men and materials up to the Arctic Coast involved the construction of a major suspension bridge over the Yukon River into wilderness territory. After making inquiries of pipe manufacturers in various countries, the contract had gone to Japan. Permission was being sought from the U.S. government as well as the state of Alaska to build the pipeline, and for permits for right-of-way to cross highways, streams, railroads and so on.

It was now that the three companies involved in TAPS encountered the unforeseen problems which nearly brought the pipeline project to an everlasting standstill. These obstacles threatened to shut off the huge oil field as completely as if it had never been discovered. Opposition delayed the start on the construction of the pipeline for five years, contributed to the cost being not $900 million but, before the whole job had been completed, nearly $10 billion and subjected the men working for the oil companies to nearly a decade of frustration.

The trouble arose from three sources: the rights of the native peoples of Alaska; opposition from the environmentalists and conservationists in the "lower forty-eight"; and the fact that the huge pipeline project was not in the hands of one operator but in those of a committee of firms whose interests were to some extent in conflict. At just that moment when ARCO discovered the biggest oil field the United States had ever known, the American people were concerned as never before about preventing business interests from interfering either with the rights of the native peoples or with the resources and environment of the United States. Furthermore, the new field required technological development beyond the experience or resources of any one American company.

Before Alaska became the forty-ninth state of the Union, it had been a territory, and as such the whole of its land was owned by the United States government. The Alaska Statehood Act of 1959 had given the new state the right to select 103.5 million acres, more than a fourth of its total area, to be held as state, or public, land. At the time of the Prudhoe Bay discovery this had not yet been done; there had been no great need for haste. Now that there was, the selection still could not be made until another provision in the new statehood law had been carried out. The statehood law prevented the state from selecting for its public sector any land which was claimed by any of the three native populations: the Eskimos, Aleuts and Indians. The native peoples had been in no great hurry to make their selection of land until, in the mid-sixties, they saw the oil companies coming into the state and acquiring leases. As sales increased, the natives protested to the federal government in Washington and asked the secretary of the interior to prevent the governor of Alaska from granting further leases. In 1966, Secretary of the Interior Stewart L. Udall ruled that no more federal land was to be transferred to the state, and

Hugo Anderson and Hilda Nelson shortly before their marriage in 1914.

Robert Anderson in 1938.

Barbara Phelps in 1938.

he Malco oil refinery, 1942.

Opening the first Wilshire gas station, 1957.

The chairman of Malco Wilshire, 1957.

At the Port Arthur Refinery, Texas, 1965. On the right is Dow Hamm. (*Photo: J.C. Watkins*)

A well head, or "Christmas tree," at the Prudhoe Bay oil field, Alaska, ca. 1969. Bob Anderson is fourth from the right.

At an Aspen Institute awards ceremony honoring Willi Brandt, 1974. The Stetson was a gift from Bob Anderson. (*Photo: Berko, Aspen*)

With Shahbannu Zahedi of Iran, Aspen, 1975. (*Photo: Berko, Aspen*)

Relaxing in the Marble Garden at Aspen. The garden was designed by
Herbert Bayer. (*Photo: Berko, Aspen*)

Barbara and Bob Anderson
on the Circle Diamond ranch.
(*Photo: Bruce Davidson/
Magnum*)

Bob Anderson and Paul Ravesies sign the offshore drilling agreement with the Chinese in the Great Hall, Beijing, 1982. (*Photo: William F. Clark*)

that no more oil or gas leases on federal land were to be granted until all native land claims had been settled. This was the situation in 1968 when ARCO made its discovery on the North Slope.

"The discovery of that oil was greeted with enthusiasm in Washington," recorded Bob Anderson. "Udall and the Department of the Interior were delighted. They saw, naturally, what benefits that oil offered to the native of Alaska—and to the United States. We were on good terms with Udall—he knew us, we knew him—we anticipated his cooperation. We knew about the embargo on land transfers and the native land claims, but these were being dealt with—expeditiously, we thought—and we were given to understand, definitely, that they would not stand in the way of us getting on with the continuation of the pipeline. I'm confident that if ARCO could have gone in right away, told the government we would begin to build the pipeline the following day, we would have been given permission to do it—it was a routine matter—at worst we would have been granted a temporary or conditional right of way, to stand in principle, but maybe subject to demands for modifications and rerouting. But on our part we didn't want to rush in—there seemed no need, and there was a great deal to prepare. So while we didn't start to build the road at once, we began immediately and without inhibition to order miles of pipe at considerable expense and to move in the men to survey a route for the right-of-way."

What ARCO did not understand at the time was that while relations between ARCO and the Department of the Interior in Washington were good, the same could not be said of the relations between Washington and the state of Alaska. In 1968 Secretary Udall was in conflict with Governor Walter Hickel over the federal lands issue. In November of that year came the presidential election. The Democrats were turned out, the Republicans came in. Hickel was a Republican. It is said that on hearing that Governor Hickel of Alaska was going to succeed him as secretary of the interior in Washington, which Hickel did, Udall made an observation similar to, "Well, I'll make sure he doesn't rush into doing the wrong thing"; or, another report, "I'll teach that son of a bitch a lesson." What is not gossip is that in his very last hours of authority as secretary of the interior, Udall extended the embargo on land transfers for another two years. As a consequence of this, the start on ARCO's pipeline had to be post-poned for two years.

But much worse was to come. The pipeline became caught up in a far bigger issue—the environment, conservation and pollution. This issue converted what might have been a two-year delay into a five-year delay, and drove up the cost from the $900 million originally estimated to the $5 billion estimated when construction of the pipeline began in 1974—a figure far below what would turn out to be the final bill.

For several years in the 1960s, long before the discovery of the North Slope field, concern about the environment had been steadily mounting and had become a prime issue of national politics. There had been special interest in Alaska. Reports in 1968 that an eight-hundred-mile pipeline would be built across its virgin mountains created a sensation. In August 1969 public hearings were held in Alaska, and these were followed by others before Senate and House committees in Washington. They were attended by Alaskans, as well as by many representatives of bodies that had never been to Alaska. Some of the testifying Alaskans were ardent conservationists; others were much more interested in getting the oil flowing, and the profits into Alaskan welfare schemes, than in protecting the caribou and the bears.

In the course of the hearings the Department of the Interior issued a proposed set of technical and environmental stipulations which would accompany any permit issued for the building of a pipeline. David Brower, the founder of Friends of the Earth, complained to the senators that these stipulations had loopholes "you could float the *Manhattan* through" [the *Manhattan* was a 1100-foot oil tanker]. In spite of Brower's strictures it looked as though permission to build the pipeline would be given. The Trans-Alaska Pipeline System repre-sentatives did their best to answer all charges and deal with all queries. The Department of the Interior was helpful. Toward the end of the year, in spite of the pressures of the conservationists, some of the ARCO men thought the permit to build was on its way. The new secretary of the interior, Walter Hickel, and his deputy, Russell Train, seemed to think that, at any rate, work on the supply road could begin. In December the TAPS staff experimented by building a 2250-mile ice-log bridge across the Yukon. Its project manager thought that official permission to build the pipeline was only six weeks away.

He was wrong. In 1969 an event, much publicized at the time, was to have profound consequences on public opinion. An oil well off the coast of California in the Santa Barbara Channel began to leak oil into the ocean. Before anything could be done to stop it, damage had been done to wildlife and to recreational facilities. There was a national outcry. In his State of the Union message the following January, President Richard Nixon spoke of the need for the preservation of the environment.

Simultaneously the new National Environmental Policy Act went into effect. Intended to provide safeguards for the environment against any project that, if permitted, would stand on or cross federal lands, the new law required that before any such project could be permitted, an "environmental impact statement" about it must be submitted by the Department of the Interior. This statement was to be accompanied by a list of alternatives to the project and by evidence that these alternatives had been studied. The "environmental impact statement" would be based on the information the department obtained from those who had proposed the project and from other interested parties. "I think the first environmental impact statement was a couple of pages long," Bob Anderson recorded, "but the final version filled twenty-six volumes."

In March several conservationist organizations, including the Friends of the Earth, the Wilderness Society and the Environmental Defense Fund, filed suit in Washington's federal district court, alleging that the number of yards of right-of-way being requested by TAPS in Alaska contravened the Mineral Leasing Act of 1920. The court responded by issuing a preliminary injunction preventing the pipeline from crossing land at Stevens Village on the north bank of the Yukon. The following month the environmentalist groups also proceeded against the Department of the Interior under the new NEPA Act, alleging that the department had not complied with the "environmental impact" provisions of the new act. This, too, led at once to an injunction preventing the building of the supply road. As though for good measure the native rights' lobbyists now weighed in: two native villages which a few months previously had signed waivers to allow the pipeline through their property now withdrew the waivers, complaining that the promise of jobs for their inhabitants on the project had not been honored. Five other villages filed suits to prevent the Department of the Interior from allowing either road or pipeline to proceed. By June the whole gigantic enterprise was stalled. TAPS began to put thousands of tons of equipment and materials into mothballs, where the great bulk of it was to remain for the next four years.

The environmentalist and conservationist organizations were of different kinds. Some of them—which Anderson approved of and supported—had existed for years, such as the Conservation Foundation, the Audubon Society, the Wilderness Society and the influential Sierra Club. But in 1969, with the realization that the environment could be made into a big political issue for the 1970s, some new organizations were spawned of which he was suspicious: "They seemed to me to be more interested in using the environment as a means of reducing public confidence in the government than they were in the environment itself. Others, I thought, were selfish: they wanted to preserve vast sections of land for themselves rather than open it to the public." Bob found that some organizations, once they understood what ARCO proposed to do—and realized that ARCO shared their consensus and was ready to act on their advice—dropped their opposition to the building of the pipeline. He found, too, that some leaders of environmental organizations did not want the pipeline built at all, but were trying to score the political victory of having prevented its construction. Others adopted stances which, though honorable, were non-negotiable. "One leading environmentalist," recorded Bob, "stated after a several-day conference with ARCO in Alaska that while he thought ARCO could and would build a pipeline which would be environmentally acceptable, he would continue to oppose the pipeline because he didn't want any more oil coming into the United States, especially California, until the people of California learned how to live properly with their environment.

Well, did he expect ARCO to teach environmentalism to the people of California before we could move oil down there from Alaska? Apparently he did."

The problems created by the environmentalists were compounded by a third factor: ARCO was not in sole charge of the operation. TAPS was run by a committee of, at this time, three, and later eight oil companies. There were divisions on the committee: whether the pipeline should go underground or aboveground, or if some sections should be above, others below; how long the different sections should be; and where they should be located. In August 1970, TAPS disappeared and the pipeline enterprise was incorporated into the new Alyeska Pipeline Service Company, a nonprofit contractor whose purpose was to design and build, and then own, the pipeline. The shareholders were ARCO (28.08 percent); SOHIO (Standard Oil of Ohio, of whose 28.08 percent a quarter was held by British Petroleum); Humble, a subsidiary of Exxon (25.52 percent); Mobil (8.68 percent); Union Oil (3.32 percent); Phillips Petroleum (3.32 percent); and Amerada Hess (3 percent). "It would have been better," said Bob, "if the building of the pipeline had been in the hands of one company. The men in a company know each other and work with each other. Even if they do not like each other they are used to each other. But here were three or four big companies supplying men to work together who'd never met before. And each company had different ideas of doing things and of what should be done. It was very unsatisfactory. We did it that way because no company wanted to leave decisions to any other company, and because there was an assumption that the job was too big for any one company to do."

There was another unfortunate aspect of the partnership. At the outset Exxon did not have the same interest as ARCO in hastening production to the North Slope. ARCO was short of crude, whereas Exxon was receiving large supplies of crude from the Middle East. British Petroleum, on the other hand, having lost its crude in the Middle East, wanted to get its hands on crude from the North Slope wells. Exxon had no wish to hasten British Petroleum's entry there. In March 1969, Bob Anderson met with the president of Humble, representing Exxon, and Walter Hickel, then secretary of the interior.

At that moment $75 million worth of Caterpillar trucks and tractors were on the banks of the Yukon ready to start building roads and laying pipes on the other side. "I wanted to get them across and Wally Hickel wanted to get them across, but the president of Humble said that he had misgivings. We all knew that in three weeks or so the thaw would begin and we wouldn't be able to get them over the river anyway. We had just those three weeks in which to move. I wanted to get them over and risk whether we got a permit. Wally Hickel was all for it. But the president of Humble would not agree to put them on the other side until the permits to build the supply road were actually in their hands. Humble finally gave in and we moved everything across the ice in the next few days. By the following summer the whole project was halted by the clamor of the environmentalists. Those trucks stayed on the far side of the river for five years without moving. It cost us millions just to keep their engines warm and serviced."

The new Alyeska Pipeline Service Company spent 1971 largely on paperwork and countless trips to Washington. The paperwork included the first draft of the Department of the Interior's "environmental impact statement" as required by the NEPA legislation—196 pages, accompanied by another 90 pages of revised construction stipulations. "This was the beginning of the most frustrating five years of my life," says Bob Anderson today. The committee also studied a scheme for abandoning the pipeline and moving the oil from Prudhoe Bay in a fleet of 170,000-ton nuclear submarine tankers which would move under the ice and deposit their cargoes at a port in Greenland, where a deepwater harbor could be provided (according to Dr. Edward Teller, the nuclear physicist who had helped to produce the first atomic bomb) by blasting one out of the ocean by means of nuclear explosions. Walter Hickel was a strong advocate of forgetting about a pipeline and extending the Alaska Railroad to the North Slope, moving the oil from the slope to the port by means of tank cars. The use of a monorail was canvased. So was the building of an eight-lane highway to carry vast fleets of trucks, until it was pointed out that such an operation would require nearly all of the trucks being currently used throughout the entire United States. Boeing and Lockheed examined schemes for flying the oil out of Prudhoe Bay in jumbo jets. Another ridiculous suggestion was to build a pipeline large enough in diameter to contain a track on which tractors could carry the oil away in drums. Many interesting suggestions arrived at Alyeska's headquarters from individual scientists, most of them amateurs. One was for a pipeline containing fluid on which the oil could be floated the eight hundred miles or so to Valdez in aluminum foil containers. Others suggested hurtling it through the air in cans on a cable, as money used to be banged about overhead in department stores. There was no shortage of suggestions.

Bob Anderson summed it up: "So we had two problems, and one of them would have been more than enough. We found the oil just before the environment became a national political issue: the Alaska pipeline was cast to be the first case; we were the guinea pigs for the new legislation. And the second problem was that the pipeline, the biggest commercial undertaking in American history, not just the most costly but physically the biggest, had to be built by a committee. We had to devise a suitable organization; we had to bring together the right people from several different countries to fill the posts; and we had to form a management for it—all this in the knowledge that these arrangements would be dissolved when the pipeline had been built."

The first break in the legal logjam came in December 1971. After many debates, committee sessions, amendments and compromises, the Alaska Native Claims Settlement Act of 1971 (ANCSA) became law. Among other things it gave the natives the right to select 44 million acres of land. They would relinquish any further land claims in exchange for a payment of $462 million over a period of eleven years, plus a 2 percent mineral royalty until they had been paid an additional $500 million. After these concessions were made to Alaskan natives, the federal government lifted the embargo on the sale of federal land to the oil companies for the construction of a supply road and a pipeline.

This did not mean that ARCO could immediately put its plans into operation, since all the environmental lawsuits remained. The Department of the Interior was now being inundated with demands from environmentalists that an alternative to the pipeline be considered, the so-called Canadian alternative. This was a scheme to build a pipeline to take the oil eastward from Prudhoe Bay across the Canadian border into the delta formed by the Mackenzie River flowing northward into the Arctic Ocean.

Nearly six months went by before the "Canadian alternative" could be ruled out. Among the many objections to it was that since a trans-Canada pipeline would be at least three times as long as the one originally planned there would be a much greater hazard to wildlife. The expense of constructing it would be at least three times as great. Before the oil could arrive in the United States it would have to pass across the territory of a foreign country which could turn the tap on or off at will, or which might prove indifferent to, or incapable of, taking proper measures for the protection of the pipe.

Congress did not relish the fact that it had been saddled by the Supreme Court with the responsibility for dealing with the pipeline; the question of the dimensions of the right-of-way for a road had become embedded in highly charged issues of native rights and environmental protection. Every congressman knew that the voters had no great love for the oil companies; now the Supreme Court had presented Congress with the complex and unwelcome problem of whether or not to permit the authorization ad hoc of a hundred-foot right-of-way instead of a fifty-foot right-of-way for the Alaskan pipeline. Congress knew it would have to act, but it was in no mood to act quickly.

As it happened, Congress was forced into action by events. Five years after the oil had been discovered at Prudhoe Bay, when not a yard of the pipeline had been constructed, there was a great clap of thunder in the Middle East. On October 6, 1973, the Yom Kippur war broke out. Egypt and Syria invaded Israel. The United States government declared that in view of the unprovoked aggression, it would send military aid to Israel, whereupon Saudi Arabia and the other members of the Organization of Petroleum Exporting Countries (OPEC) ordered a total embargo on shipments of oil to the United States and a cutback on production. The United States was immediately faced with a fuel crisis. It suddenly became imperative that the North Slope oil begin to flow. Congress terminated its debates abruptly; two weeks sufficed to resolve all difficulties. The trans-Alaska pipeline was legally authorized on November 16. Work on the supply road began at once. Some of the environmentalists felt that they had not gotten as many guarantees as they should have. Some thought they had done as well as could possibly have been expected. Some continued to protest that the pipeline should not have been permitted. But they all had to face two facts: there was a national fuel crisis; and Congress had spoken loud and clear.

The construction of the pipeline proper began in the middle of 1974. About 360 miles of it was to be conducted underground at a depth varying from 3 to 12 feet, and nearly 400 miles of it was to be aboveground at varying heights. The aboveground sections would be carried by vertical support members (VSMs), 78,000 of them each costing as much as a Cadillac, set up in pairs and standing at intervals along the route varying from 50 to 70 feet. About 50 miles of the pipe would be buried at depths requiring refrigeration for the pipe so that the hot oil would not create temperatures which would melt the frozen ground around it. At several points the pipe was specially designed and constructed to comply with the conditions laid down by the Department of the Interior. For example, at twenty-two points along its route the pipe was taken under the ground for about a hundred feet to meet the conservationists' complaint that caribou and moose would not pass under a raised pipeline: "dipsy doodles," the pipe constructors named these underground sections. In total, and at vast expense, eight hundred animal crossings were constructed. Most of them proved unnecessary: it soon became clear that moose and caribou had no inhibitions about passing below the pipe; they liked to stand under it to enjoy the warmth. It had been said that many of the animals would be so frightened by the sight of the pipe that they would forsake their haunts to get away from it. The reverse usually proved to be the case. The Dall sheep came down from the mountain to look at it. Wolves were leery to begin with but soon began to prowl around the construction camps, where workers succeeded in feeding some of them by hand. Bears, including sows and their cubs, followed the pipeline into the camps or into the drilling stations, without fear, looking for food.

As a precautionary measure a number of bears were rounded up and flown to a suitable location about a hundred miles away. In a few days they found their own way back to the camp from which they had been moved. Biologist Kenneth Durley, supervising the effects of the building of the pipeline on the fauna of the area, reported, "You can tell the conservationists that we're not giving the bears any problems . . . the bears are giving *us* problems."

Caribou grazed placidly beside the airstrips and took shelter from the summer sun under the raised buildings at the campsites. White fox and red fox played among the lengths of pipeline waiting to be laid. Geese, swan, loon and tern kept up their annual migrations to the North Slope. The salmon ran in the rivers as before. Snow geese, never previously seen in the area, arrived in 1971 and started nesting. Angus Gavin, a distinguished Canadian wildlife expert, had been asked by ARCO to make a six-year study, from 1969 to 1975, of the effects the construction of the supply road and the pipeline were having on the flora and fauna of Alaska. "It is quite evident," Gavin reported, "that these operations have had little or no effect on the normal activities of the wildlife that frequents this part of the Slope."

The pipeline was ready to take oil in midsummer 1977. The estimated cost of it was now a little short of $8 billion, though again, this later had to be revised upward. The thirty construction camps were closed down one after the other. On August 1, 1977—nine years after the oil had been discovered—the ARCO tanker *Juneau* sailed from Valdez full of oil. Bob Anderson's goal—to make ARCO absolutely independent of any company at home or abroad for its crude ("the heart of the matter")—had been achieved. The dependence of the United States on foreign sources of oil had been reduced by between 15 and 20 percent. It was a remarkable achievement, but at a great price.

"The cost of the delay to ARCO and the oil companies was one thing," said Bob Anderson, looking back on it all, "but the cost to the United States and its friends in the West was another. If we had been allowed to proceed with the building of the pipeline, giving reasonable guarantees of native rights and for the environment—and we would have had no difficulty in providing these, none whatsoever—

so much would have been different. By 1973, when the Yom Kippur war broke out, there would have been so much oil coming out of Alaska that there simply wouldn't have been a world fuel crisis. The OPEC countries could have done what they liked—for America, Great Britain, France, Germany, Italy, Japan, all the other countries outside OPEC, it would have been business as usual. There would have been no appreciable rise in the price of oil. As it was, when OPEC established the embargo the price of oil went up from less than $3 to more than $11 a barrel overnight. If there had not been that delay over starting the pipeline, if the oil had been coming down from Alaska, there would not have been that sudden inflationary rise in world prices whose effects are still with us today. It was tragic."

The experience had enormous consequences for ARCO as well. As Mo Benson recorded about the climate of public opinion at that time, "All of a sudden, we in the oil industry weren't just disliked, we were hated." Said Bob, "The experience taught us that, given ARCO's size and given developments in social consciousness, ARCO must behave as a *political,* as well as commercial, organization and always have an eye to its social role—political in the broadest sense of the term. Perhaps 'civic' is a better word. We could no longer think of ourselves only as a decent company producing decent oil and giving decent service. We were now deep into environmental affairs, pollution issues, conservation, consumer needs, political considerations and so on. And to deal with this new dimension of activities and responsibilities we had to develop new functions."

CHAPTER SEVEN

Telling the story of Bob's progress as an oilman has taken us well beyond one of the most formative events of his life. Let us go back to 1953 when, at the age of thirty-six, he made his first acquaintance with the now internationally known Aspen Institute for Humanistic Studies, named after its location, the resort town of Aspen, Colorado. But first a quick look at what the Aspen Institute is, and does today, thirty years after Bob Anderson began to work on it.

The Aspen Institute has come a long way from its birth in 1949. Its main endeavor is to bring together, sometimes for a couple of days, sometimes for a week, sometimes for two weeks, some of the ablest and most informed men and women in the world to discuss, with a view to trying to solve, the most critical problems of our times, in such areas as government, education, industrial relations, the arts, the media, health and agriculture. The hope of the institute is that from the ideas and observations exchanged by such people *around* a table, there may emerge a consensus which can constructively influence government, industry, education and private as well as public organizations. The aim of the institute, as stated by Bob Anderson, is to be "a catalyst by which people who make decisions can convert ideas and values into action." The Aspen Institute is independent, nonpartisan and nonprofit, as well as international and neutral. It is supported financially by various foundations, including the Ford and Rockefeller foundations; by tuition fees paid by those who attend its business seminars; by subscriptions from individuals and corporations; to some extent by grants from national and international governmental and other public organizations; and mostly by Bob Anderson. It is run by a small permanent staff headed by its president and directed by a board of thirty-seven trustees, program directors and special advisors.

The activities of the institute are threefold. First, ten or twelve times a year, it conducts Executive Seminars: a dozen or so business executives get together for about two weeks with distinguished teachers, and on the basis of study of selections from the books of the great thinkers of the past and present, apply ideas and values to modern society in general and their own experience in particular. In essence, the seminars for the businessperson are refresher courses to stimulate and broaden thinking, and to question the conventional wisdom. When Bob took over the institute, these seminars were its only function.

The second activity of the institute is the conduct of a number of long-term programs, extending over the years, each a series of conferences and discussions in various areas of social activity, bringing to light problems of critical concern. The long-standing program on Communications and Society aims to improve the standards of performance, mobilization of talent, content, diversity and outreach of the mass media. Other programs include Education for a Changing Society; Science, Technology and Humanism, which examines how science can work as a humanitarian as well as a utilitarian force in society; International Affairs, consisting of a series of discussions and conferences covering a range of issues from arms control to the poverty of the underdeveloped communities in the Third World; and Environment, an outgrowth of Bob's personal interest in the subject. The Environment program was discontinued in the early 1980s because the institute had concluded that a number of newly created organizations were giving adequate attention to environmental problems. All programs embody the same working principle: "Thought leading to action."

A third main activity of the institute, its newest, is conducted under the title of Governance. A series of conferences and discussions sustains an examination of such topics as how societies and lheir governments and institutions, public and private, national and international, can better respond to the conflicting pressures of social justice, fairness, efficiency and individual freedom.

Although the Aspen Institute was founded in 1949, the ideas which sprang from it dated from the year before. In 1948 three eminent Chicagoans had decided that something should be done to encourage the postwar rebirth of intellectual life in Germany and to bring the German people back into the cultural embrace of the West.

The occasion for the launching of their effort, these three men decided, would be the bicentenary of the birth of Johann Wolfgang von Goethe in 1949. They planned an international convocation of scholars and men of letters at the University of Chicago. Two of the men hoped that the event would give support to an already existing program, which they had devised, for University of Chicago professors to accept teaching assignments at the Goethe University in Frankfurt. This scheme was the brainchild of one of them, Professor Giuseppe Antonio Borgese, professor emeritus of Italian at the University of Chicago. Borgese was also a German scholar. He had come to Chicago from Rome, driven out by Benito Mussolini, in the mid-thirties. The chief supporter of his scheme, the second member of the trio, was the chancellor of the University of Chicago, Robert Maynard Hutchins. The third member was not an academic but a businessman, Walter Paul Paepcke, of Germanic origin, founder and head of the Container Corporation of America. Though not an academic, he was involved with the University of Chicago because he had married Elizabeth Nitze, the beautiful and talented daughter of a professor at the university and sister of the distinguished American ambassador Paul Nitze. Paepcke became deeply interested in education and the arts and was a trustee of the University of Chicago, a trustee of the Chicago Orchestral Association and patron of the Art Institute of Chicago. A passionate lover of music, he was a devotee of the Salzburg Festival.

If this bicentenary was to come to anything, Paepcke knew, he would have to finance it. Encouraged by his wife, he decided to do so. The three men agreed that the bicentennial gathering would not use the occasion merely to pay conventional homage to Goethe, but to use his life and work as terms of reference for discussion of the state of the contemporary world. Paepcke agreed to finance the great event, on two conditions: that the centenary celebration should include a music festival comparable to that of Salzburg; and that the convocation of scholars and musicians should be held away from any great city, in a little town high in the mountains of Colorado, a community and a locale which in some respects resembled his beloved Salzburg, and which he loved to visit: Aspen.

Walter Paepcke had visited Aspen for the first time only two years previously. He found it a dilapidated, ramshackle town: its Victorian houses, most of them uninhabited, needed paint and repairs; the charming old hotel, the Jerome—built by Winston Churchill's grandfather—was falling to pieces bit by bit, like icing from a crumbling cake; barns looked shabby and forlorn; and the streets were empty. Paepcke, a man of vision, saw Aspen as a potential American Salzburg, given its location in this mountainous grandeur. He resolved to create one. Such an Aspen/Salzburg would need an economic base, so he began to buy land and houses and to plan tourist attractions which would bring in money. To begin with, he formed two companies, first the Aspen Company, to make the Jerome Hotel a profitable enterprise, and to develop eighteen real-estate holdings; and, secondly, the Aspen Ski Corporation, to provide one of the best ski areas in America. He told the town leaders what he proposed to do to restore and develop the town, and urged them to invest, on the Swiss and Austrian model, in retailing goods which would be bought by visitors: woodware made of the local Aspen tree; jewelry made of Colorado silver; woolens, milk, cheese and butter. He proselytized his friends from all over the United States to come to Aspen for a healthy and/or cultural holiday.

In making these plans for the development of Aspen, Walter Paepcke put much reliance on his friend Herbert Bayer. Bayer had been a distinguished member of the Bauhaus, the now legendary school of design founded in Weimar, Germany, in 1919 by the great

German architect Walter Gropius and devoted to training students in aesthetics related to technical craftsmanship. The name of the school, "house of building," came from inverting the syllables of the word *Hausbau,* meaning "building of a house." Walter Gropius's purpose in founding the Bauhaus was to produce artists who over a period of years in the workshops would qualify to become craftsmen. The divine urge to create was to be yoked with the knowledge of how to do it—inspiration was to be wedded to know-how. In 1933 the Bauhaus was closed by the Nazis and Gropius went to the United States. In 1937 a new Bauhaus spread its wings in Chicago, later to be known as the Institute of Design.

Bayer, an Austrian, also left Germany. Arriving in the United States with an international reputation as a typographer, graphic designer, architect and painter, he became a consultant to Paepcke in Chicago, executing commissions for Paepcke's Container Corporation. The men soon became friends, and Paepcke urged Bayer to come to Aspen, live there for several months in the year and redesign the town as an American Salzburg. "You are an Austrian," Paepcke said to him. "You know the mountain towns. Build a Salzburg in Colorado. You can do it." Bayer considered the pros and cons of leaving New York, and finally made up his mind to go to Aspen as designer-in-chief of the new Aspen Company, with a seat on the board.

The Goethe bicentennial festival opened on June 27, 1949, and lasted thirty days. There was a magnificent music festival in a tent, designed by Eero Saarinen, which housed a full symphony orchestra and an audience of 2000. Arthur Rubinstein was only one among a galaxy of world-famous performers. Thinkers and artists came from all over the world to participate in the Goethe program, including Albert Schweitzer and José Ortega y Gasset. Among the Americans, Thornton Wilder was prominent. The excellence of the music festival and the high-caliber intellectual discussions were widely reported in the American newspapers. As the last day of the bicentennial approached, the question on everybody's lips at Aspen was: "Why can't this great occasion be repeated?" Though the festival had left Paepcke some thousands of dollars out of pocket, he resolved that somehow the festival must be made an annual event.

From his resolution in December 1949, the Aspen Institute for Humanistic Studies was founded, the title and purpose owing much to Ortega y Gasset. It had two functions: to run a permanent music school and produce an annual music festival, and to conduct in the summer months a series of seminars at which top industrialists, business leaders and scholars would discuss selections from the fifty-four-volume set of *Great Books of the Western World*. In Paepcke's words: "It is not the aim of the Aspen Executive Seminars to make a better treasurer out of a treasurer, or a better credit manager out of a credit manager, or to show how an advertising vice president can be more effective in promoting a product. The aim is to help American business leaders lift their sights above the possessions which possess them, to confront their own nature as human beings, to regain control over their humanity by becoming more self-aware, more self-correcting and hence more self-fulfilling." Though a substantial fee was to be paid by all participants, or by the business corporation that sent them, the institute had to be subsidized from the first by the profits Paepcke made from his Aspen real-estate holdings and his skiing company. In 1950 the seminars were held on premises in the town hired for the occasion. In 1953 Paepcke decided the seminars needed a permanent home and commissioned Bayer to build a conference center, the Aspen Institute.

Aspen soon became very expensive. The financial pressures proved more than Paepcke had bargained for. He could look with pride across the United States and count the number of institutions being developed on the Aspen model, and he could read with a sense of achievement the press clippings which reported the impact which Aspen had made on American intellectuals. But pride and praise did not pay bills. The profits Paepcke made from his skiing company and his real estate were not enough to defray expenses; he had to subsidize the institute out of his own pocket. By the mid-fifties, Paepcke seriously questioned whether he could continue to fund an annual deficit.

In the fall of 1953, Barbara and Bob Anderson looked around for a place where they could take the six children for a good long holiday—somewhere cool, with fishing. They went to Aspen for the first time to see if it would suit them. They took Parlor B in the Jerome Hotel, the only guests at the time. Bob knew that an institute had been established at Aspen, that it was much praised, that it had close ties to the University of Chicago, and that many of his friends were interested in it. That was all he knew about it. As a businessman, and particularly as a native Chicagoan, he had heard of Paepcke but had never met him. Looking back, he recorded: "Barbara said at the end of our stay, 'You know, Bob, this would be a great place to bring the children for their summer vacations. There's plenty for them to do, riding and fishing, the mountains, skiing in the winter, and then there's the music, and the interesting people who come here.' When she said that, it struck me that just as my father had exposed us to the campus at the University of Chicago, our children might benefit from the ambience of Aspen."

On the last day of their vacation, Bob and Barbara drove around the town to see if there was a suitable house to rent or for sale. Outside a Victorian house built of red clapboard was a "For Sale" sign. They knocked and a woman came to the door. Yes, the house was still for sale. She called her husband, who came into the living room from his studio. "He was one of the most handsome men I had ever seen," said Barbara. "He was tall, dark and slim. He was wearing a canary-yellow turtleneck jersey." This was Herbert Bayer. "He was rather diffident, but charming, and Joella was warm and lively. We stayed for tea. They told us the price they were asking for the house, and that they were selling because Herbert was building a house on Red Mountain and they hoped to winter in Sicily. They had received several offers for the house, but they had refused them. Herbert was not hard up, and he had a strong feeling for Aspen. He was going to sell only when he found a suitable buyer—"a potential Aspenite." The Bayers knew nothing about the Andersons, and the Andersons knew nothing about the Bayers. They talked.

Herbert told them about Paepcke. Bob told them that he and Barbara had attended the University of Chicago. Herbert recorded: "I soon felt that these were the right people to have our house. Bob said he wanted to bring his family to Aspen and expose them to the learning and music of the institute much as his father had exposed his children to the atmosphere of the university—they would be free to take it or leave it. I thought, This is the kind of person we want to settle in Aspen, somebody who might actively help the institute. So I offered him the house at a good price." An hour later, Bob and Barbara left Aspen and began the long drive home to Roswell. On the outskirts of the town they decided to buy the house. Bob stopped the car beside a public telephone and rang the Bayers. "Is the house still for sale?" It was. "Well, it isn't anymore."

Shortly after the Andersons moved into their new home, Bob was hailed by a tall, confident man who introduced himself: "I'm Walter Paepcke; you're living in Herbert's house." After that they met many times. To Paepcke it seemed a happy stroke of fate that there should come to town a wealthy, influential and enlightened man, so sympathetic to what the Aspen Institute stood for, and so much in touch with the city and the university that had generated the ideas which the institute embodied. For Bob the turn of the wheel was just as felicitous: here on his new doorstep was the intellectual and cultural life with which he had been brought up and to which part of him had always longed to return. "I'd already realized that at thirty-six years of age, I could *not* go back to the university and find the excitement and stimulus I had known there at twenty. I was too old. I'd been around too much. I'd have found the university too slow. But Aspen held out the prospect of reestablishing my relationship with the academic world. It could provide everything a return to the university could give, but in a much more flexible and eclectic way. Aspen seemed the answer."

Bob was deeply impressed by Paepcke's objective, to create a humanistic sense of purpose in top managers and to put them back in touch with the eternal values on which Western civilization was based. He and Barbara became Aspen converts. The following summer, while their children rode horseback, swam and tramped the mountains, Bob and Barbara sat in their first seminar. To give as much time to Aspen as possible, for several weeks Bob transferred his New Mexico office to the Jerome Hotel. At the end of that summer, he joined Aspen's board of trustees. He and Paepcke soon became close friends and associates.

The arrival of Bob Anderson on the Aspen scene was a greater godsend for Paepcke than he could have realized at the time. He was suffering many frustrations, not all of which were financial. Music and the musical side of Aspen were Paepcke's greatest loves, but the Aspen musicians were giving him a lot of trouble. In his ambition to make Aspen a musical center worthy of comparison with Salzburg, Paepcke had made the mistake of creating two functions which soon became two factions: the annual festival and the newly created School of Music. "Walter was partly to blame," said Bob. "He had rather a Byzantine way of running things. He wasn't averse to blurring lines of responsibility and authority, and keeping everybody slightly off balance. And he wanted to run the orchestra himself. He wanted to choose the conductor every year and he wanted to choose the music, which was something that he did superbly. And he wanted to have new talent coming into the orchestra every season, which didn't go down with the existing artists who wanted long-term employment."

Matters came to a head in 1954. In an attempt to eliminate the conflict, Paepcke fired the director of the music school, who retaliated by inciting both orchestra and school to revolt. As a result, the musicians and Paepcke parted company, the musicians setting themselves up in a professional organization called the Music Associates of Aspen. Following this crisis in Aspen's affairs, Bob's commitment to the institute emerged. Looking back on those days, he recalled:

Walter carried on for a couple of years as though nothing had happened. But it had been a bitter blow for him. His favorite child had turned its back on him, forsaken him. It was the musical side of Aspen which had interested him—and it had interested him passionately. The nonmusical side, the Executive Seminars program, did not have the same attraction for him. That was Mortimer Adler's child. Walter supported Mortimer wholeheartedly, but he never identified himself with the seminars the way he did with the music festival. Secretly he grew very bitter about it in the next two years. In fact in 1957—we were close friends by then, and he used to confide in me—he suggested to me that we dismantle the institute and wind up the seminars, and simply have a couple of dozen eminent scholars and political leaders, leaders of industry, out to Aspen, for talks and discussions on current themes. I told him, "Walter, you can't quit.

And anyway, what you've started here is too important to give up." He said, "If that's what you think, *you* take it over." And that's how I succeeded him as president—reluctantly.

Having taken over responsibility for Aspen, Bob took a good look at its problems. As well as the problem of finance, there was a lack of organizational structure, the result of Paepcke's unchallenged personal authority—after all, he paid the bills—and of Paepcke's disinclination to involve his board of trustees effectively: in fact, they had not formally convened in eight years. Bob soon saw what had to be changed, but could not work out solutions until he had activated the board. Fortunately, over the four years the two had been associates, Bob had been well briefed by Paepcke, who alone knew the ins and outs of Aspen's affairs and kept the details in his head (there were practically no records at the institute). More difficult for Bob was the fact that the men permanently involved in Aspen were not businesspeople; they were teachers, writers and scholars, by nature individualists, not team workers, sensitive if not self-centered. Order, administrative efficiency and financial solvency did not interest them so long as they were free to pursue their creative activities.

The first thing Bob decided to do was to eliminate all activities and properties which were unprofitable, were not worth the time and trouble involved, or were not central to the real function of the institute. Aspen Airways, for example, had been set up by Paepcke to service the growth of the town. It was now running at a loss. Bob sold it to a local company. The Health Center was also unprofitable; it was relieved of an unwieldy, underemployed staff and scaled down to a size which met the demand. To increase its economic viability, the Executive Seminars program was extended into the winter, becoming more of a year-round activity.

From the first, however, it was clear to the discerning eye that Bob's conception of what the Aspen Institute ought to be was different in some important respects from that of Paepcke and the founders. Like Paepcke, Bob was totally committed to Aspen's dedication to the humanities, with the special role of reconciling them with the sciences. Like Paepcke, he believed that the institute had a mission to

provide stimulus and refreshment for top-level business and industrial leaders, to renew their contact with the experience and values of
their days at a university or college. But the conceptions which the
two men had of the role of the institute as a whole were different.
Under Paepcke the institute had been strongly oriented toward Aspen
and the state of Colorado. Bob, on the other hand, saw a potential
outreach for the institute far beyond the regional community, and a
need for it to become national and international in its scope. "The
peaceful almost pastoral world of the 1950s is light-years away from
the hectic 1980s," he said recently. "We no longer have the luxury of
viewing almost any major problem as one of our own." What he did
share with Paepcke was the conviction that the institute should be
kept small and lean; there should be only a couple of dozen or so
participants sitting down together at any one time, and the permanent
staff of the institute should be minimal.

From the first Bob had plans for Aspen which would add significantly to its functions. These plans were regarded with suspicion by
some of the first-generation Aspenites. It was clear to them that Bob
felt that the institute was too concerned with personal experiences,
personal problems, personal behavior; that he thought it should be
outward-looking and address itself more to national and international
problems. Although he wanted the seminars to continue using read-
ings from eighteenth- and nineteenth-century political writings and
from the broader outreach of philosophy, he also asked for meetings
of scholars and businesspeople to discuss special projects of urgent
present-day significance—for example, educational reforms, new
economic thinking, environmental issues, problems of modern government. He wanted to see more of the application of discussion of
eternal values to the practical problems of contemporary society. In
his youth, he had moved out of the academic world, much as he
revered it, because he found it too remote from everyday life. He
wanted to bring Aspen and its academic values with him, trying to
have them influence public knowledge and public policy. Sensing
this, some of the founders became nervous.

Then in 1960, a little more than two years after Bob took over as
president, Walter Paepcke died of cancer. His death was the signal for

the first debate about where the future of the institute lay. Should it change or should it stay as it was? And there was still the pressing problem of finance. Some of the forward-looking trustees, who were for change, suggested that to achieve economic viability the institute might set itself up as a conference center which could be used by national organizations whose objectives were essentially educational or related to those of the institute. All were agreed on one point: the institute could not survive at this stage if the Executive Seminars were not well patronized. That year the seminars' registration reached a record 112.

Bob Anderson continued his move to broaden Aspen's activities. The institute, he said, must use its unique ability to address emerging social and economic problems. He was supported by Walter Orr Roberts, a distinguished scientist and an Aspen trustee. Anderson and Roberts quickly made ground: it was agreed that the institute would appeal for a grant to the National Science Foundation, with which it would present a series of one-week seminars on the theme "The Public Understanding of the Role of Science in Society." This topic, of Bob's own choosing, was one of his main concerns at the time. "The public interest in, and understanding of science," he told the trustees, "is not commensurate with the importance that science has attained in our social structure. We need to understand more clearly that what science contributes to the national purpose is measured by what it adds to the sum of human knowledge." The grant was forthcoming. The series of seminars was launched. There was henceforth no looking back: Aspen had moved in a new direction.

Bob's determination to get Aspen more related to public affairs was much fortified, coincidentally, by the election of John F. Kennedy to the presidency in 1960, the same year in which Aspen had agreed to Bob's plan for scientific seminars. Kennedy's campaign slogan had been "Let's Get America Moving Again." The national scene was now one of change and innovation, in which the application of technology and science to social problems was one of its most prominent features. The initial seminar, "The Public Understanding of the Role of Science in Society," held in Aspen in October 1961, set a pattern for the next five years. In attendance were humanists, scientists, business leaders, university executives, trade union leaders, clergymen, newspaper editors and top government officials from both civil and military departments of state. The first series of seminars were pronounced a great success. They also had consequences—the practical effects on society which Bob had hoped for—in that these original Aspen discussions helped prepare the ground for the creation of the National Endowment for the Humanities. Meanwhile, a flow of information and ideas, generated in the Aspen seminars, permeated the United States Senate and House of Representatives. Aspen was beginning to apply its wisdom to the day-to-day problems of society.

The problem of paying Aspen's bills remained unsolved, and Bob Anderson continued to foot the bulk of the annual deficit. In November 1964, Bob became chairman of the Board of Trustees and Alvin Eurich succeeded him as president. Eurich set about tackling the financial problem at once. Consulting the records, he found that for the period 1951–64 more than 400 corporations had participated in the Aspen Executive Seminars, and more than 2000 "alumni" of the Executive Seminars now held what might be loosely termed "leadership positions" in business, labor, government, the professions, universities, and in the arts and sciences. He began a drive to raise funds from those who had benefited from the institute. He persuaded the trustees to create the Aspen Society of Fellows. Their number was to be limited to a hundred. It was a privilege to be asked to become a fellow and help with Aspen's work, but it was also made clear that an Aspen fellow was expected to help with the financing of the institute.

These successful departures, however, did not solve the ever-pressing problem of money. The institute continued to rely heavily on annual subsidies from Bob. At the end of 1966 Eurich told Bob that at sixty-five he felt he had done as much for Aspen as he could and that the time had come for him to return to educational work in New York. He formally announced his resignation at the next meeting of the trustees. Bob was not present. Eurich also told the trustees that money was still a problem, and that Bob Anderson had now reverted to the original idea that Aspen, instead of trying to go it alone, should consider forming a close association with a college or university. This precipitated an acrimonious debate, as the Old Guard restated their "pride of authorship" in Aspen and their fears that in such an association Aspen would lose its pristine identity, and its essential focus on Aspen and the state of Colorado. At the next trustees' meeting later in the month, December 1966, there was further tension when Eurich put forward Bob's "request" for a balanced budget, so that, as Eurich put it, from then on "the institute would be placed upon a sound financial basis without major support from one person for the first time in its history." There were even stormier waters ahead. Bob had become increasingly disturbed by the stubbornness of the Old Guard of trustees in insisting that the orientation of the Aspen Institute must be toward the citizens of Aspen. The trustees knew full well that Bob had been trying for years to get Aspen to do just the opposite and look to the world outside. He consequently wrote a letter to Eurich, making it clear that if disagreement on this issue persisted between him and the trustees, he would sever his connection with the institute.

For the time being, Bob humored the dissidents among the trustees. He persuaded William Stevenson, a man devoted to the original purpose of the institute, to succeed Eurich as president. Stevenson, in accepting the post, stipulated that he would hold it for only a year, or perhaps two, and on the distinct understanding that a search for a suitable long-term successor would begin at once. Special projects would be abandoned and the staff would be stripped down to a minimum to relieve the financial burden of the institute. From now on the institute would confine itself to the Executive Seminars for Businessmen, which had been its original raison d'être.

Stevenson was elected president in May 1967. His two years in that post were not easy. He had no difficulty with the local trustees, who had supported his election. The trouble came from outside. In 1968–69 nonprofit and charitable institutes and foundations came under considerable public scrutiny. In Washington, congressmen decided that all such organizations should be examined for tax purposes. Left-wing critics claimed that the foundations enabled their benefactors to indulge their whims—and obtain benefits—with tax-exempt dollars which should have been paid to the U.S. Treasury to finance measures to deal with urgent social problems. Right-wing critics alleged that these tax-evading dollars enabled organizations to promote the ideologies of radicals and socialists. Some critics, on both Left and Right, denounced foundations for using their funds, and their publications, to lobby Congress and government officials in support of legislation and policies in which they had an interest.

A long public debate led to the passage of the Tax Reform Act of 1969. The new law gave and it took away. One of its most controversial provisions was an ambiguous one which addressed itself to what was called "the legislative activities" of foundations. While permitting foundations to make available "the results of non-partisan analysis, study, or research," the act did not make clear what was meant by the term "non-partisan." The conference committee of the House and Senate stated that the law was not meant to prevent the study of broad problems which at some future time might come before the government, but it also stated that "lobbying on matters which have been proposed for legislative action" would not be permitted. This raised the question: What was the difference between putting useful facts before congressmen or government officials and *lobbying?* Governments and foundations would frequently be interested in the same national problems. How could they be kept apart? Was it not proper that a first-class examination of a problem might influence the thinking of a congressman or government official? Once the law had been enacted, in spite of its ambiguities and lacunae, the controversy about foundations much diminished. While it raged, back at the institute the debate about the future of Aspen had continued.

The great turning point, indeed the point of no return, came in 1969, when Bob appointed a new president, Joseph E. Slater. The old Aspen of the founders did not disappear—far from it—but the new Aspen Bob Anderson was trying to bring about began to occupy the foreground. On a prodigious scale there began the expansion and diversification which is going on today.

Slater was an intellectual, but his role before, during and after the Second World War was to apply learning to public affairs. Between 1945 and 1948 he had helped to plan and establish the economic and financial directorates of the Four Power Allied Control Council in

Berlin. In 1949 he joined the staff of John J. McCloy, who had been appointed U.S. High Commissioner for Germany. Slater organized the office of, and then became, the secretary-general of the Allied High Commission. Among the other offices he has held are chief economist to the Creole Petroleum Corporation in Venezuela and director of the Ford Foundation international program.

In 1968 Slater had become chairman and president of the Salk Institute for Biological Studies. By now Bob Anderson had set up the Anderson Foundation through which he could channel his financial support for all his philanthropic activities, including the Aspen Institute. That year Bob offered Slater the presidency of both foundation and institute, along with the freedom to remain chairman of the Salk Foundation, and to use the two Anderson organizations to further its work.

Slater had spent a summer at Aspen as a resident scholar while he was with the Ford Foundation, and he had learned a good deal about the institute. He admired some aspects of it, but deplored others. He said so to Bob. "I told Bob that the offer he had made me was tremendously flattering and overwhelmingly generous, but that the most honorable way to respond to it, the most complimentary way to him, was to tell him the truth. First, if I got stuck with the Aspen Institute as it was, and had to move from New York to Aspen and live in that inward-looking intellectually incestuous atmosphere, I'd be suffering from cabin fever from the start and would be no good to him or to myself. You can't get involved in a constructive effort to have an influence on world affairs and hope to run the show from a little holiday resort way up in the Colorado mountains. If you want to try and influence people with power, you've got to go where people of power hang out, *go* to their surroundings and *work* with them in their surroundings. I also told him that I didn't think enough of the institute's activities were international and I was only interested in being international. I also told him—and I wondered how he would take it but I just had to tell him—that the Executive Seminars for Businessmen simply wasn't a viable program; it was worthy, but it simply wasn't worth an institute. I just didn't see why you needed all that Aspen setup, all those facilities, for *that*—you could get all that done by a committee. And I wasn't interested in arranging for the physical accommodation for an institute based on those seminars and negotiating with the Aspen community for more land to provide facilities for conferences; I didn't want to get into the real-estate business. Above all, I said, I couldn't stand burying myself in an inward-looking little outfit like Aspen is today. When I got to the end of that spiel, I thought to myself, Well, that's that, Joe Slater, if you ever wanted that job you've talked yourself out of it. But not at all. Bob said, 'Joe, if you had said you wanted to leave New York and set up house in Aspen I would have withdrawn my offer to make you president. And everything you say about the institute is right. Just go away and put down on a page or so of notepaper what you would like to do as president of Aspen if you took the job. Give me a five-year Action Plan 1969–1974. Give me the answers to these four fundamental questions: Which functions of the institute should be continued, which dropped? Which are in need of revision and strengthening? What adjustment to policies and programs is necessary in view of the changes in the world outside since the institute was founded in 1949? What kind of financial and operational structure would best enable that institute to carry out its proper role?' "

The terms of reference given to Joe Slater for his action plan would have appeared at once to anybody familiar with the arguments of the last few years as a brief to pull Aspen out of the past and set it moving—and moving fast—in the direction for which Bob Anderson had been pressing. Meanwhile, before Slater left, Anderson agreed to back him in establishing, independently of Aspen, a new international institute for the study and solution of world environmental problems, later to become the International Institute for Environment and Development.

The two men agreed to meet as soon as Joe had written down his action plan. As Slater saw it, "From the word Go we were now planning for a truly international institute. Second, we were agreed that the institute had to work on a year-round basis—how could you tell people you were going to deal with the problems of the world only in the summer? Third, we were going to deal with the great pressing life and death issues of our time. Fourth, if we felt that any program we had inaugurated was not getting results we would bring it to an end. Fifth, we should always be bringing the humanities, and their values, into whatever subject we were discussing. Sixth, and this was very important to us, we would get the best-qualified people in the world to look at the bewildering nature of change itself—the change in weaponry in a nuclear age; the alienation of young people; the intractability of racial problems; the alienation of the individual in urban societies; the problems of food and energy which involved conflicts; the communications explosion; the biological explosion; the population explosion. And that's the way we've gone. I met Bob in Los Angeles a few days after we first talked. Bob said, 'Did you put those ideas down?' And I said, 'Yes, I now have a five-year Action Plan. It comes to less than a whole page of paper.' 'That's fine by me,' he said. I passed it to him across his desk and he read it. He didn't say anything—just wrote 'Okay. ROA' and the date. That's his style.''

Bob and Joe worked hard and fast on the Action Plan. Having thought it out, they costed it out. They put it before the trustees of the institute, verbally and in writing, at the end of December 1969. It was unanimously approved. The Action Plan consoled the conservative trustees by declaring that the humanities had become more important than ever as technology, and the tendency to materialistic thinking, had become more dominant in modern society. There was more, not less, need for such a function as the business seminars, ever the core of Aspen's purpose; the continuing involvement of "men of affairs" in the Executive Seminars must "remain the central activity of the Institute," and must have the first claim on its attention. Indeed the institute's Executive Seminars "were bound to be more important in the future" than they had ever been, since in the new mood of criticism "all governmental, political and business systems were being profoundly questioned."

Most innovative was Joe's list of six new programs, very much the twin product of his own and Anderson's thinking. They amounted to a new constitution for the institute. As submitted to the trustees they were: Communications and Society; Environment and the Quality of Life; Education for a Changing Society; Science, Technology and Humanism; Justice and Society; and International Affairs. Bob

Anderson explained to the trustees that Slater, with his outstanding experience of the foundation world, and with his prestige as an impresario in public affairs, would do his best to enlist the interest and aid of the big corporations in all of Aspen's activities. He would enhance the work of the institute by linking with like-minded organizations overseas. He would mobilize all possible assistance from outside to enable Aspen to operate with the smallest possible administrative staff.

The Action Plan succeeded. By the end of the five years he had set for it, Slater, while preserving and strengthening the core of the enterprise, the business seminars, had widened the reach and range of the institute's activities almost out of recognition.

In 1970 Slater appointed journalist and former presidential advisor Douglass Cater to lead the program entitled Communications and Society. The program gave great critical attention and publicity to the government's inquiry into the effect of television on crime and violence, on "anti-social behavior by individuals, especially children." There were conferences and papers, on a variety of subjects, including authoritative publications by Cater on public broadcasting, and in particular how, against the intense competition of commercial radio and television, the American Public Broadcasting Service, a conglomeration of "community stations," stations licensed to local school systems, states, municipalities and universities, could solve the all-important problem of finance. Cater also organized a series of seminars on the theme "The Government and the Media." Increasing attention was paid to government policy involving the Federal Communications Commission, Office of Telecommunications Policy, Congress, and several other government and nongovernment agencies involved. Another series of conferences during the early seventies was devoted to the subject of television as a social cultural force.

Among many other problems, Slater organized in 1973 a conference in Washington, D.C., which was in essence a briefing for senators and congressmen on revolutionary developments in biomedical medicine and the implications of these for future legislation. Aspen also launched itself on extensive programs of international affairs discussion. Under a new program of "Thought Leading to Action" launched in March 1975—Pluralism and the Commonwealth, directed by Waldemar Nielsen—Aspenites and assembled experts discussed the effects of the growing influence, in great part for financial reasons, of government on learning, education, research and scientific innovation. The purpose of the program was to alert the public to these developments, and to try to provide an answer to the problems. This was the kind of "Thought Leading to Action" which Bob hoped to see more and more frequently: humankind taking notice of an urgent problem brought to its notice by the Aspen Institute.

By the end of 1975 the Aspen Institute had come a long way from what it had been in Paepcke's day. Indeed, it had come a long way since Joe Slater took it over in 1969. It was not just that all the "Thought Leading to Action" programs were under way, but that, while the original function and character of Aspen had remained unaltered, the seminars were now the core of a wider operation which to many seemed more important, as well as more visible. Accordingly, while Aspen still had its premises in the Colorado mountains, it also had headquarters in several other parts of the world to serve its many new worldwide activities. Its operational headquarters were in New York. Its programs were directed from such outposts as Palo Alto, California; Princeton, New Jersey; and Washington, D.C. There was an Aspen Institute in Berlin, there would soon be one in Hawaii, and before the seventies were out, another in Maryland, near Washington, D.C. During the last few years, owing to differences with Aspen city officials, the institute has been selling its property, conducting more and more sessions at different locations away from Aspen, and building up its base on the eastern shore of Maryland, at Wye Plantation, just outside Washington, D.C.

Some idea of what happened to Aspen under Bob Anderson's stewardship is conveyed by its annual program. Twenty years ago its calendar would have listed a maximum of five businessmen's seminars of two weeks each, taking place at intervals in the summer months. The 1986 calendar lists nine seminars at Aspen of the traditional kind—they are described as "Traditional Executive Seminars"—but includes another eighty institute meetings or conferences, most of them lasting three or four days, several of them being held at Aspen or Wye, but most of them overseas, at such venues as Berlin, Paris, Rome, Capri, Turin, Istanbul, Oxford, Tokyo and the island of Hawaii. The list of topics indicates the change in the terms of reference on which the institute now works, as these random samples might suggest: In January, there was a discussion at Wye of "Public Policy Issues in Energy and Resources"; at Canisy, France, on "The Great Challenges for France in the Next Ten Years"; and in Berlin on "New Dimensions of Security." In February at Wye, in the program "Justice and Society," there was a seminar on "Law and Literature"; at Sea Mountain, Hawaii, a meeting on "Energy Demand and Energy Prices"; and in Rome a seminar on "International Technological Initiatives."

The most famous of the institute's recent achievements has been its preparation and publication in December 1984 of a document on "East-West Relations: Past, Present, Future," now regarded as having made a powerful contribution to the easing of tension between the Soviet Union and the United States, which was later to be expressed by personal meetings between President Ronald Reagan and the Russian leader Mikhail Gorbachev. The East-West report's analysis of the state of tension, with practical recommendations about how it could be reduced, was the result of conferences held in Washington, Berlin and Venice of groups of statesmen, diplomats, and military and civilian experts; many of the sessions were chaired by Bob Anderson.

This great transformation of the nature and reach of the Aspen Institute for Humanistic Studies has now been accepted by many who knew what the institute was like when Bob Anderson succeeded Walter Paepcke in 1957. It was the very inwardness of Aspen, the retreat for a couple of weeks from the pressures and preoccupations with the outside world, which they saw as the Aspen mission. For some of the purists of those happy fifties, and no doubt for Paepcke, with his prime concern for music, Bob has taken Aspen away from what it was intended to be.

Paepcke, with his thoughts of Salzburg, saw Aspen as a Mecca to which people would come to refresh and fortify themselves, then, strengthened, go back into the world and go about their business with a new light in their minds and a new energy. Bob sees Aspen not only as a retreat or a holiday from the world, but also as a force by which the world which we cannot hide from can be changed. Paepcke wanted to be the impresario of an essentially cultural and private activity in a beautiful resort in the Colorado mountains. Bob Anderson wants Aspen also to be the creator and director of a fund of knowledge, experience and information which flows daily through the world of politics, policy and power, and hopes that "the continuing dialogue" and exchange of ideas which Aspen seeks to promote may help to improve the individual human condition.

CHAPTER EIGHT

Among the many and various international organizations working today for the preservation and improvement of the worldwide environment two are outstanding: the International Institute for Environment and Development (the IIED) and the International Environmental Bureau (the IEB). The leading figure in the foundation and financing of both was Bob Anderson. The newer of the two, the IEB, a specialized division of the International Chamber of Commerce, was established in 1986, by which time the world had become well aware of its environmental problems. The IIED, on the other hand, was founded in 1970, when public opinion still needed to be mobilized and educated in environmentalism, and when concern about the mounting hazards had not been matched with the will and expertise to deal with them.

Bob's encouragement of the environmentalist movement, particularly in the early days, was not welcomed by some of his peers in the oil and gas industry, nor by some of his associates. As early as 1969, ARCO published in its annual company reports critiques—not all of them favorable—made by outside experts of its attempts to maintain a high standard of conservation, and it made grants to a number of environmentalist organizations. Though he disapproved of some of his views and tactics, Bob helped Dave Brower to establish Friends of the Earth. Long before that he had been a pioneer of the environmentalist movement through the Aspen Institute. But the origins of his concerns are not so much a response to the pressures for preservation and improvement built up by public opinion, nor of his own spontaneous sense of responsibility as an industrialist for not doing damage to the environment. Rather, they are the expression of that love of wildlife and the countryside growing out of walks as a boy with his parents through the fields and woods around Chicago. He told a gathering of ecologists three years ago:

> I don't know when exactly I became an environmentalist, but I think it may have been one day as a small boy I dug up a spadeful of pretty good loam. Like the odor from new-mown hay the scent of a good loam is unmistakable. There is something unique about the smell of the earth. No manufactured perfume can capture its fragrance. I remember that day. When I was young, it seems to me when I look back, all my family and friends were naturalists. Later a buzz word came along—conservationist. Now, in the last twenty years or so many of us call ourselves environmentalists.

Bob's institutional contributions to the environmental cause began twenty-five years ago when he encouraged Walter Orr Roberts, a solar astronomer, then director of the National Center for Atmospheric Research, to organize an international interdisciplinary conference at the Aspen Institute, co-sponsored by the National Academy of Science, the National Research Council, the High Altitude Observatory and the Air Force Research Laboratory. The conference assembled in 1962 and featured participants from a wide range of countries. Its object was to clarify the relationship between climate and nutrition. The same year, the institute began a series of summer meetings in Aspen, co-sponsored by the National Science Foundation and Colorado College, for the benefit of high school biology teachers interested in ecology. Both conferences made considerable contributions to what the institute planned to do in the field, and indirectly prepared the minds of the experts for the great surge of public interest in ecological and environmental issues which was about to begin.

In the same year Rachel Carson published *Silent Spring*. A marine biologist with a gift for writing, she had previously written such books as *The Sea Around Us* and *The Edge of the Sea*, in which she combined scientific knowledge with creative prose. She had acquired a great following. Now, in *Silent Spring*, her main message was of the danger from weedkillers and insecticides to human beings and wildlife. Concern for the environment escalated. In September 1963, President Kennedy addressed the General Assembly of the United Nations and called for a great effort in which all the countries of the world would strive "to defend the human environment, to protect the forest and wild game preserves now in danger of extinction, to improve the marine harvest of food from our oceans, and prevent the contamination of air and water by industrial as well as nuclear pollution." Scientific approaches to the problem occupied more and more attention at Aspen. In 1968, Bob was asked to address a conference in San Francisco, held under the auspices of the United Nations. In his speech, entitled "The Blue Planet," he reminded his listeners that when the American astronauts had returned from the most recent space visit they had described seeing the earth from space as "a perfectly beautiful brilliantly blue sphere, but rising from it, if you saw it in the morning sun, an unquestionable crescent of ugly smoky haze." Something had to be done about that, said Bob. He used as his text the story of what had begun to happen to the common land of England three centuries before.

> The Common in the village belonged to everybody, so everybody grazed their sheep on it. If anybody wanted to put a few more sheep on it, they were free to do it, and did it. So the land deteriorated, because though everybody owned it nobody took responsibility for it. Will we learn that lesson? Today our atmosphere is common to us all, our seas are so many commons, like the lands of England three centuries ago. Much of our water resources are common. Yet we have not learned how to manage these great collective assets, all now in danger of running down, and so far only a relatively small number of people are considering their responsibility for what is happening.

In 1968, Aspen President Joe Slater suggested to the Swedish ambassador to the United Nations that he put a proposal before the

General Assembly for a U.N. conference on the environment to be held in Sweden, a country known to be concerned about environmental issues. Bob and the Aspen Institute would help. The proposal was accepted and the conference would be held in 1972.

In 1969 Slater presented Bob with his six action-oriented programs as the core of the institute's work over the next few years, and with Bob's enthusiastic support put them to the trustees. One was entitled "Environment and the Quality of Life." For basic information and thinking about this program, Joe consulted Thomas W. Wilson, who, soon after the National Environmental Policy Act had become law in 1970, began a study to be published under the title, *International Environment Action: A Global Survey*. Funded by Bob Anderson, Wilson finished his book in four months. Its first chapter was published as a pamphlet by the Aspen Institute in the summer of that year under the title, "The Environment: Too Small a View." The pamphlet had an unexpectedly large circulation among government officials, politicians and leaders of opinion, and excerpts from it appeared in newspapers and magazines. The institute followed with a conference of international scientists, economists and historians to consider the social and ethical aspects of world environmental problems which Wilson had set out in the Aspen pamphlet.

As a result of the vigorous support for the environmental cause expressed in his annual reports as chairman and chief executive officer of ARCO, Bob had already been identified as one of the few American business leaders who fully, publicly and articulately recognized the industrialist's duty to help solve the world's environmental problems. In November 1969 he was invited to deliver another address in San Francisco, this time to the United States National Commission for UNESCO. In his speech he expressed the essence of his position as an environmentalist: there was a role for protest, but the most important need was for constructive action, and protest must never get in the way of that. As he put it on one occasion, "It is more fun to fight than to reason, but it is by reason ultimately that we shall get things done." He told his audience:

I know of no more important business for all of us than the environment and the manner of our interacting with it.

Many people who have become aware of the growing crisis have arrived at an angry, even despairing, state of mind. They tend to see modern man as stupidly condemning the soil to erosion, blindly exploiting the forests and the seas, mindlessly polluting the air and waters, recklessly fouling the countryside, and the cities as well, driving to extinction one species of animal life after another. This anger and despair rest upon a gloomy assessment of man and of what motivates him.

Perhaps anger is helpful, even essential, in arousing us all to action. However, it can also inhibit the constructive approach we need for what well may be the greatest of all problems for contemporary society.

Bob then went on to suggest some practical action that might be taken, including expanded research and development of anti-pollution technology: a national program to study the reduction or elimination of air pollution from waste and exhaust fumes; greater use of materials that deteriorate naturally (the so-called biodegradable materials); new techniques for recycling waste products, along with new criteria for determining what is "economic"; education of private companies and consumers as to unnecessary packaging and the disposal of unused waste; legislative and judicial regulations on the question of liability for damage to the environment when it occurred; and an all-out attack on noise pollution, "for it constitutes possibly the greatest of all intrusions on personal privacy."

The speech in San Francisco was given a great deal of publicity, not all of it favorable. Many industrialists thought it so much pie in the sky. Many in the oil industry resented his criticisms and felt he was surrendering to the environmentalists. Some liberals thought he was being hypocritical, others Machiavellian. On the other hand, many praised him. "When one of the nation's top corporate executives says in a major public forum that we had better start shifting our sights from quantity to quality," wrote Gladwin Hill, the environmental specialist of *The New York Times*, "an historic corner plainly has been turned." He was right. For several years, Bob's seven recommendations figured on the agendas of practically every serious environmental organization in the country.

Over the next few years Bob was to state his view of the proper approach to the environmentalists many times. It always came down to the same simple proposition: "We must face the fact that there is going to be protest. We must face it, welcome it, and do everything we can to educate that protest so that it can be constructive." To demonstrate his faith that this could be done he established RESOLVE, an organization devoted to urging the resolution of environmental disputes without resort to legal action.

By now ARCO, in addition to its sections in the annual report, was producing special reports on its responsibility for protecting and enhancing the environment, and describing its efforts to discharge it. An excerpt from one of them particularly reflects Bob's own views:

Pollution. The word is as familiar and repugnant to most Americans as the reality it represents: foul air and water, littered countryside, noise, ugliness and decay. Until recently, we considered these blights the inescapable by-products of growth and abundance. But are they?

Through more than 200 years of industrial revolution many people have accepted the proposition that the earth's resources—from the minerals within the planet to the envelope of air that surrounds it—are limitless. The result was often a ruthless exploitation of these assets with a resultant decline in the quality of life. Streams became murky, the atmosphere grew opaque, the landscape eroded and died.

By mid-twentieth century, reality intruded. We discovered there are not only limits to our resources, but that we are perilously close to reaching them, especially those of water and air. And it began to dawn on us that, as pollution afflicts us all, the responsibility for its cause and cure must likewise be shared by all—from individuals to giant municipalities, from mom-and-pop enterprises to multinational corporations.

The petroleum industry is no exception. By the nature of their far-flung activities, oil companies have a high potential for injuring the environment. From wellhead to gasoline pump, the complicated process of converting fossil fuel into usable energy presents numerous ecological challenges.

To what lengths can a modern technological society pursue the dream of a pollution-free environment?

Most of us realize that the excesses of the past must not continue, but we know also that a return to a pristine yesterday (which was not so pristine anyhow) is not possible. To heed such proposals is to wreck the economic base upon which rest the needs of millions of Americans who suffer the worst kind of pollution—that of poverty. The disregard of human privation in housing, health and education violates the tenets on which our nation is based. Clearly a balance must be struck, assimilating the aims of both environmental protection and economic growth.

Atlantic Richfield is convinced these twin goals—high environmental quality and a viable economy—are compatible. This conviction is born of nearly a century of trying to meet our obligations to conserve natural resources and accept the expense of protecting the environment. Atlantic Richfield's commitment is set forth in our Environmental Protection Policy. Its objectives can be achieved only if every operating employee understands and is trained in the ways he must contribute to these goals.

Since 1969, when the company issued the first of these reports on its stance in the environmental struggle, there have been many changes and much progress. Much of it, we must acknowledge, resulted from official spurs—the inexorable public pressures that lie behind most advancement in a democracy. But much of the progress was ours, pressed by an awareness that each of us must do our part—that leadership in an industrial context means more than numbers in a ledger.

And beyond what one company, or one industry, can accomplish, tangible results in reclaiming a deteriorating environment truly depend on a cooperative commitment by private citizens, government and industry alike.

Meanwhile, preparations for the 1972 Stockholm conference were under way. In 1970 began an active three-way exchange of ideas between Maurice Strong, United Nations under–secretary general in charge of environmental affairs, as well as the conference's executive director; Thomas Wilson; and Bob Anderson. Strong realized that he had many problems ahead of him. Knowing that it was difficult enough to get governments to deal with their own national environmental problems, he knew how much more difficult it would be to get them to agree to plan and act with each other. A realist with personal experience of how politicians and civil servants operate, he took the view that the Stockholm conference would not be productive unless the delegates were furnished well in advance with a broad conceptual framework for their deliberations. Furthermore, they should be given specific areas of discussion on which agreements could be reached. Strong did not expect that the conference would solve any of the major problems; what he hoped for was agreement on a program of work for the future. Thinking out such a program could not be left to begin at the conference; guidelines and suggestions for it would have to be presented to the delegates well in advance. Its preparation, he became convinced, could not be entrusted to any of the existing governmental or international agencies, certainly not the U.N. Secretariat, understaffed and inexperienced in this field, and imbued with conventional thinking. It would have to be done by somebody else.

Thinking hard along these lines, Strong came to two conclusions: if the Stockholm conference was to have the requisite preparation, he would need the services of somebody who really understood the world's environmental problems, had the knowledge and experience to organize nongovernmental groups and influential individuals, was capable of bringing a specific, relevant, practical and assimilable program before the conference for its consideration, and had the resources to distribute it to the delegates in advance. Secondly, Strong concluded, to carry on the good work when the conference was over it was essential to create a new international organization in the U.N. system, which would not only be far more effective to that end than any existing agency but would be specifically designed for it.

For the first, Strong went to Thomas Wilson. For the latter, he went to Joe Slater. There was a meeting of the minds. The plan was right: now for the power to make it work. They went to Bob Anderson. The result was the establishment in 1970 of the International Institute for Environmental Affairs. Its raison d'être was to help Strong with the Stockholm conference; furnish it in advance with information, ideas and agenda; get it to agree to a program of practical work for the future; and from then on to give continuing guidance as to how the program could be implemented and to provide a lead to all organizations and individuals on the environmental problems of the world.

The new institute's philosophy and purpose were described as follows:

Because of the unitary nature of the biosphere, many environmental concerns are inherently trans-national. What is global has application to a locality; what is local has impact on the globe. Constructive efforts in environmental affairs must be international in scope and—most important—multidisciplinary in approach.

Moreover, such efforts must be sustained, for there are no "solutions" to our environmental problems—only the hope and necessity of managing them on a permanent basis. Fundamental efforts to deal with problems of the environment must go beyond nature conservation and pollution abatement. They must transcend technical and legal measures for PROTECTION of the environment, and must serve to ENHANCE the health and harmony of relations between man and nature on a global basis.

What distinguished the IIEA from most other organizations at the time was, as its statement of purpose went on, "the underlying assumption that concern for the quality of the human environment ultimately must engage the attention of the entire world community"; that environmental protection constituted "a common enterprise of such scale and ramification as to place it alongside international efforts to keep world peace."

In yet another distinction, which a few years later was reflected in the change of name of the IIEA to the International Institute for Environment and Development, the statement also noted:

It is demonstrable that some environmental problems are rooted in industrial and technological development. Others are rooted in a LACK of development. Still others are shared by societies in various stages of economic growth. Thus priority tasks of extraordinary political and psychological complexity emerge:

- to manage our relations with Earth's environment on a multinational basis and in the interests of the entire human race; thereby in the interest of each of us.
- to maximize the unifying effects and to minimize the divisive effects of our new ecological awareness.
- to accomplish these by stimulating the full flow across international boundaries of information that will enlarge our still limited understanding and action in coping with environmental problems.

The new institute would do everything which Strong wanted done, and much more. Bob and Joe Slater had already moved a long way in their thinking about what Aspen could and should do in the cause of the environment. They had been struck by the valuable work done in the field of defense by the Ford Foundation, based in London and funded by the Institute for Strategic Studies, and had been wondering whether a comparable institute under the auspices of Aspen could be established for equally authoritative and influential studies of environmental issues. Maurice Strong had knocked on their door for help at a most propitious moment. Bob not only agreed to put up the seed money for the establishment of a new body to do in the field of the environment what was being done for the Institute for Strategic Studies in the field of defense, but he also decided that his support for the new institute should be private, and that therefore its funds should come from the Anderson Foundation, his personal trust. He also decided that the new institute would be independent of Aspen but would have the responsibility for carrying out the Aspen environmental program. Those Aspen trustees with relevant expertise would assist the new organization in its early stages and continue to help it in any way they could. The new institute would operate on the Anderson principle: "that environmental problems should be solved by education rather than adversarial attitudes."

A suitable person was required to head the new organization. It occurred to Joe Slater that an experienced journalist with many international connections might well make a good head for IIEA. When he served with the Allied Control Council in Berlin he had seen a great deal of Jack Raymond of *The New York Times*, and formed a high regard not only for his reportage and comment but his grasp and judgment of international affairs. Raymond, in the course of a distinguished career at the *Times*, went on to serve as correspondent for the Balkans, based in Belgrade, then correspondent in the Soviet Union and finally as defense correspondent in Washington. Following two reporting stints in Vietnam, Raymond had left journalism in 1966 to join an international public relations firm. He had for a long time been interested and active in the environmental cause, not so much from scientific interest but, in the context of long-standing experience of international affairs, seeing it as a problem of intergovernmental relations and of conflicting national interests. When Joe Slater talked to him about Bob's plans for the creation of IIEA, therefore, Raymond was extremely interested and soon became its first president.

Raymond's first task, particularly with an eye to preparatory work for the Stockholm conference, was to recruit a board of directors which, given the role of IIEA, had necessarily to be international. It was decided that there would be two co-chairmen: Bob, and Roy Jenkins—as Jenkins dryly observed at their first meeting, "an oil baron and a socialist." One of the four top men in the British Labour Party, Roy Jenkins was a figure of great international standing, a fact which he underscored later when in 1976 he was elected president of the European Community.

Once IIEA was formed, Maurice Strong, as executive director for the coming conference, formally asked that the institute help 'the United Nations with the preparations. His invitation was criticized. Several U.N. bureaucrats objected to his alleged high-handedness in reaching over their heads and enlisting an outside private body to carry out this important work as though the U.N. staff was not competent to provide the infrastructure. Strong was not perturbed. He knew what he was doing, and why, and pressed on with his plans.

In these early days what he wanted most urgently was what he defined as a "conceptual framework" for the delegates' deliberations. Originally he had thought that this might be produced in the early days of the conference as a result of discussion among the eminent experts who would be attending. Wilson soon persuaded him that this would not work: any delegate might well be wedded to ideas for discussion which would be incompatible with those of other delegates. If all delegates were invited to suggest a "conceptual framework" when the conference opened, he said, no conceptual framework would emerge and "the result would be a shambles." Bob, with some experience of conferences, in particular the Environment conference at Aspen, entirely agreed. Wilson then made the following suggestion: "The conceptual framework should be laid out first in a draft manuscript written by no more than two collaborating authors. At the same time, we can set up the most distinguished group that can be found to serve as consultants who will review and criticize the draft by correspondence. In that way," Wilson said, "We can have the contributions of the world's greatest experts without having to bring them together in one place." Strong agreed. Bob suggested, "And we'll publish it as a book."

What had been conceived as merely a sensible plan for providing a conceptual framework for the conference thus became a much greater and more influential enterprise. The World Bank and the Ford Foundation offered to provide the financial support. The influential British journalist and economist Barbara Ward (Lady Jackson) and Professor René Dubos, the American bacteriologist, agreed to write the draft text. A committee of 152 experts was recruited to read and criticize it. The book duly appeared, under the title of *Only One Earth*. It was published in nineteen countries, in fifteen languages, and reached many printings. In his preface to it, Strong recorded the indebtedness of the United Nations to IIEA for its "highly effective management of a complex process with no precedent to provide guidance."

Throughout 1971 a great deal of work was done for the environmental cause. Jack Raymond got IIEA going as an organization; Wilson planned a first Aspen international environmental workshop to take place over eight weeks in the summer; Strong laid down the foundations of his conference. In April the Aspen Institute joined with the United Nations Association of the United States to host a group of Russians interested in world environmental problems. The meeting was a success. Soon the Soviet Academy invited a similar group, including Bob, to Russia. At these two informal and unofficial meetings, there was long and frank discussion of several areas in which the two countries might have mutual environmental interests and come to terms about them—the Bering Strait, for example. The time was not wasted. In 1972 Richard Nixon and Leonid Brezhnev signed a formal agreement on environmental issues.

After nearly four years of preparation, the United Nations Conference on the Human Environment finally took place in June 1972, in Stockholm's Parliament Building. It lasted for two weeks and has since been described as "the bellwether conference of the new environmental era." Attended by 1200 delegates from 110 countries, by hundreds of people representing governmental and nongovernmental agencies, and by many interested individuals, it proved to be the catalyst of many movements and organizations which had yet to be born.

The conference passed 106 resolutions. These were constituted in an Action Plan which would represent the tasks and guidelines to be adopted by governments and international organizations for the future. The plan had three divisions. The first, a global assessment program, Earthwatch, would identify and measure environmental problems of international importance and warn the world of coming crises. Earthwatch would monitor the atmosphere by means of a network of 110 specially equipped stations which would record pollution and changes in climate. Secondly, environmental management activities were prescribed for implementing measures to protect the environment. Thirdly, the plan called for educational, financial and organizational support measures. Several resolutions tackled specifically the need to deal, for instance, with fallout from nuclear tests, with industrial discharge into the atmosphere of toxic substances and with insecticides. The conference discussed the apparent contradiction between the industrialized countries' concern for the environment and the developing countries' need to industrialize themselves by methods which caused some of that concern. It also discussed the question of whether it was possible to combine rising environmental costs with increasing assistance to the developing countries. Robert McNamara, attending the conference in his capacity as president of the World Bank, gave a categorical answer: "There was no question of whether the wealthy countries can afford to combine rising environmental costs" with increased help to the developing countries. "It is clear that they can." The World Bank's studies, he said, had shown that hazards to the environment could be reduced "either at no cost or at a cost so moderate that the borrower has been fully agreeable to accepting the necessary safeguards." The work of the conference was influenced by the preparations made for it by IIEA, whose most important contribution was a resolution for the creation of a U.N. program for the safeguarding of the human environment.

The resolutions of the Stockholm conference, the Action Plan and the IIEA's recommendation of a U.N. program for the environment were submitted to the General Assembly in the form of a report, which was accepted the following December. U.N. Resolution 2997 of December 15, 1972, established the U.N. Environment Secretariat to serve as a focal point for environmental action and coordination within the U.N. system and to administer the new United Nations Environmental Programme (UNEP). Maurice Strong was elected its executive director by acclamation.

One of the effects of the conference was to raise the question of whether IIEA could optimize its potential influence worldwide so long as it was so obviously American-based and led. Jack Raymond, at a luncheon meeting with Anderson and Slater in the course of the conference, proposed that he resign and the institute's headquarters be moved to Europe. They were eventually established in London, and Raymond was succeeded by Barbara Ward. Bob later said:

> Barbara seemed impressed by what we were hoping to achieve with IIEA. So I asked her informally what thoughts she had about IIEA's future, and whether she might consider heading it up. She said, first, that the new institute should recognize that environmental problems marched side by side with development problems, and secondly she said that in this approach it was essential to enlist the countries of the Third World. "If you address yourself to the problem of the environment without working for development, you are going to doom most of the world to eternal poverty. I have a deep concern for the environment, but I see that as being consistent with my basic social concern." If, in order to embrace this approach, she said, I'd be willing to change the name to the International Institute for Environment and Development, she would head it up. I was delighted to agree to her conditions.

Over the next few years, the Aspen Institute increased its input to organizations, including those of the United Nations, working directly or indirectly on environmental problems or on projects in which the environmental aspect was important. In 1974 the institute worked out what was to be the major contribution to the preparations being made for the U.N. World Population Conference in Bucharest and for the U.N. World Food Conference in Rome. A third conference was organized to enable Maurice Strong, as executive director of UNEP, to hear the views of world experts on the relationship of the biosphere to the demands mankind's needs were making on it.

Bob, meanwhile, made several public statements relating the need to protect the environment with the conservation of energy. Some of these did not go down well with his fellow industrialists in general and with his colleagues in the oil industry in particular.

"In our extravagant lifestyle, we have been burning up our precious resources of gas and oil as though there were no tomorrow, no day of accounting," he told the Graduate Business Council at the University of Texas in November 1973. In the same year, in a speech called "Corporate Responsibility in an Open Society," he said, "We in industry have a responsiblity for searching out constructive solutions to plaguing problems." These bland words upset nobody, but he went on:

> The kind of leadership I'm talking about goes beyond self-serving statements about good corporate citizenship in advertisements and reports to shareholders. It means—and I apologize for using Atlantic Richfield as an example—analyzing a problem and taking a public stand, as we did recently on the Highway Trust Fund. The Highway Trust Fund, as you may know, is derived from gasoline taxes and earmarked principally for interstate highway construction. In our analysis of the benefits of the use of this fund—and remember that we sell gasoline and asphalt—we concluded that some of this money would better serve the nation's needs if it were spent on total public transportation systems.
>
> We concluded that portions of the Highway Trust Fund should also be allocated to transportation-related social needs, such as air pollution research, housing relocation made necessary by construction of new transportation systems, and aesthetic improvements. We arrived at these conclusions and made our recommendations known in a company position paper. We weren't satisfied merely to take a stand at the corporate level. We felt that to be effective our position had to be communicated to all levels of our work force as well as the general public.

This did not go down well with some ARCO shareholders. Not all Bob's mail was from fans.

While stepping up the supplies of money and energy he was putting into the environmental cause through and outside Aspen, Bob was at the same time trying to persuade overenthusiastic and misguided environmentalists to be more constructive in their approach. He felt that some of them in their efforts to prevent one kind of damage being done to society were causing other damage whose consequences might be worse.

There were demands of perfection for which the technology either did not exist or would cost too much to provide. He saw some environmental activists creating unnecessary difficulties. In his home state of New Mexico, he said in October 1975:

> It seems to me unfortunate that America's late-blooming concern for the environment is pitting advocates of clean air and water against those who argue on economic grounds for faster development of our energy resources, especially coal. This opposition has crystallized in the lawsuit brought by the Sierra Club against former Interior Secretary Rogers Morton. It seeks to force a new and essentially duplicatory environmental impact statement that would encompass the entire seven-state Western coal region.
>
> These legalities may not be cleared up for three or four years. Meanwhile the coal industry has fallen far behind its production of two years ago. And yet it is generally recognized that, unless we are able to double our production within the next ten years to over one billion tons a year, any hopes of escaping foreign energy domination are so much pie in the sky.
>
> Clearly the federal government should intervene. We need a nationwide policy on land use and environmental protection that will clear away these impediments to orderly development. Economic growth and environmental sanity are *not* incompatible. Extremists on both sides have made their points. The time has come to find the middle ground.

The following year he told the Council on Foreign Relations: "Concern for the physical environment is one of the noblest causes of our times. Results have been impressive—cleaner car exhausts, reviving lakes and waterways, curbs on new pollution . . . but our headlong efforts of the last half-decade to undo the environmental wrongs of the past century have produced a severe and dangerous imbalance: we are paying too much for the environmental protection we are achieving—in lost jobs, lowered productivity and lost opportunity for growth."

But in this effort to ensure that the national standard of living did not become the victim of overenthusiastic conservationism, Bob never failed to give the environmentalists their due. In a 1976 interview he was asked to reminisce about his environmental concerns during the Alaska pipeline construction, and specifically whether he had considered withdrawing ARCO's support of environmentalism when activists tried to stop the building of the pipeline. Bob's answer:

> No, we always assumed that their concerns were well-founded. We only disagreed with the way in which they were approaching the issues; their insistence on extreme responses to environmental questions.
>
> I should note that there probably was a great deal more cooperation between the companies involved in the pipeline and the environmental organizations than met the public eye. The companies did try to cooperate with the environmentalists because both sides recognized that the problem had to be resolved in a manner that would satisfy the public at large. A balance had to be struck between our nation's energy needs and environmental concerns.
>
> In retrospect, I think that in terms of a satisfactory environmental resolution, the Alaskan pipeline is the most successful project our nation has tackled. The pipeline is in operation today with a minimum of disturbance to the environment.

By the 1980s, even the most stubborn industrialists had come to recognize the desirability of new approaches to environmental protection. Out of this change of mind came the International Environmental Bureau, a specialized division of the International Chamber of Commerce. Although they became suitably alert to environmental issues when these affected them directly, large industrial concerns tended to be wary of international activities regarding environmental policies and standards. "We made a mistake boycotting Stockholm in 1972," conceded a spokeman for a major chemical concern twelve years later. Back in 1972, he explained, industry "hadn't felt the need to deal with environmental groups—many of which were just political activists. Consequently there was no industry position in Stockholm at a time when the environmentalists became institutionalized." Industry was not alone in its attitudes or in its regrets. Even the most wary governments found they might have achieved more through dialogue with industry than by flaying "the polluters." But while industries and governments were learning their lesson, neither was enthusiastic about applying it. Governments were still cautious, and industrialists, while now alert to such environmental issues as affected them directly, were nervous about becoming involved in international activities which might impose upon them environmental policies or standards which would inhibit their activities.

Though by 1982 international organizations dealing with environmental issues had proliferated, Dr. Mostofa K. Tolba, Maurice Strong's successor as executive director of the United Nations Environmental Programme, had perceived that no satisfactory ongoing relationship had been established between governments and industries. His own agency maintained useful contacts with world industry through liaison with major trade associations, but these contacts had not led to world industry as a whole committing itself to environmental action. In June 1983, on the occasion of World Environment Day in New York, Dr. Tolba said: "For the past ten years we have been trying to convert the converted—we have been talking to the environmentalists, and we have not tried to go beyond that." He then announced plans for a World Industry Conference on Environmental Management (WICEM) with the cooperation of the International Chamber of Commerce, to be held in Versailles, France, that November.

Bob was not among those first involved in WICEM, and Atlantic Richfield, although it contributed seed money to the undertaking, was not among the official conveners. But when the planners ran into some trouble, it occurred to one of them that Bob Anderson might be able to help. What was needed at that stage, he was told, was a batch of ideas for post-conference action which would focus the minds of those attending the conference and give them a prospect of how its deliberations could be carried out in practical programs. Could he supply them? The request was similar to what had been asked of him before the Stockholm conference, again for "thought leading to action." Anderson convened a summer workshop at the Aspen Institute, to which he invited some fifteen specialists from companies, trade associations and nongovernmental organizations.

The observations of the Aspen workshop were set forth in a letter by Anderson to Dr. Louis von Planta, chairman of Ciba-Geigy, the Swiss-based international manufacturers of specialized chemicals, who, as chairman of the WICEM committee, had been charged with developing post-conference action proposals. Anderson was insistent that the Aspen workshop report be considered not as a statement to the conference but as a contribution to the thinking of the committee. Dr. von Planta should feel free to accept all, part or none of it. Von Planta was impressed by the report and urged his committee to adopt the entire document.

The guiding principles shaped at the Aspen workshop and enunciated in the von Planta committee document provided a basis for the meeting of minds between Anderson, von Planta and David Roderick, chairman of U.S. Steel (now USX), when these three later met at the WICEM conference at Versailles. "A Magna Carta for environmentalism," one writer called them. They stated:

1. *Care for the environment is a common responsibility of society and should be taken account of in all activities, including industrial activities.* Mankind should continue to pursue efforts to understand the natural environment, especially to anticipate the consequences of industrial and other human activities. All elements of society must take action to minimize known adverse effects on the environment.

2. *Industrial activity should take into consideration related economic and social responsibilities.* While industry cannot ignore economic or so-called "bottom-line" realities and survive, neither can it ignore the broad needs of society and survive. Industry thus has no less responsibility for "good citizenship" than any other element in society.

3. *Sustainable economic development is a desirable international goal.* Economic development can improve the quality of life by reducing or eliminating poverty and thereby improving human dignity. In some parts of the world, economic development is the sole hope for maintaining life itself for entire populations; the profound implications of this situation for other parts of the world cannot be denied or ignored. But inadequate planning and miscalculation can be counterproductive. Development efforts should be sustainable, lest they invite economic and social disappointment as well as cause damage to the environment.

4. *Scientific and technological information is vital to environmental protection.* Government and industry should encourage the dissemination and exchange of significant information that can be shared and used, in part or in whole.

5. *Governments should promote the adoption of common goals in addressing environmental concerns.* States may have different value systems that guide environmental policy decisions that affect industrial activities. However, governments must recognize their common responsibility for global environmental protection.

6. *Governments should deal even-handedly with all industrial enterprises.* Governments should not establish environmental standards for certain enterprises that are more rigid or demanding than standards and requirements set for other enterprises, regardless of ownership or social purpose.

7. *Cooperation is more efficient than confrontation in addressing environmental concerns.* Governments are obligated to ensure the best possible environmental conditions for their citizens. Similarly, industry is obligated to meet governmental requirements in the most economic manner possible. If conflicting obligations occur in certain instances, it must be recognized that confrontation leads to the most expensive and time-consuming approach to problem-solving. Cooperative procedure must be sought to permit more widespread environmental improvements.

8. *Governments and industry should address environmental issues as early as possible in the economic planning and development process.* Experience has shown that development requires complex interdependent actions related to public policy and national strategies. Therefore, environmental considerations as well as technology, economics and marketing concerns should be factored into development plans at the outset, in order to avoid costly delays and damage due to tardy recognition of environmental consequences.

9. *Industry and government separately or cooperatively should promote awareness of environmental issues.* Ignorance is the worst enemy of a healthy environment. In too many industrialized as well as less developed countries, negative environmental factors have been recognized but addressed too long after damage was caused unwittingly through lack of information and understanding. On the other hand, environmental hysteria should be avoided. Industry and government both can contribute effective educational and informational programs for a better understanding.

10. *Cost/benefit analysis is, despite its limitations, an essential element of environmental decision-making.* Just as cost-effectiveness is the key to survival of industry, it should also be the cornerstone in national and international environmental efforts. Practical efforts

should be made to ensure that cost/benefit analysis is universally applied in environmental problem-solving.

Anderson was invited by von Planta to join in the committee's presentation at Versailles and by Dr. Tolba to address the conference's final plenary session on the same platform with the chairmen of the sponsoring organizations and the Prime Minister of France. He was the only company chief so honored.

WICEM was attended by more than 500 representatives of more than 70 countries. Its final declaration proclaimed a set of goals for achieving economic growth compatible with good environmental management and stressed the importance of disseminating information, especially to enhance the interests of developing countries.

After the conference, however, a postmortem meeting of some twenty-five representatives of various organizations at U.S. Steel's New York headquarters created the impression that in spite of all the good intentions voiced at Versailles, there was a danger that in the long run the conference might prove unproductive. A staff member representing David Roderick, chairman of U.S. Steel, who had been one of the most active participants at the Versailles meeting, said, "Nothing will happen unless chief executive officers get involved." Jack Raymond, representing ARCO, drew Roderick's man aside and asked, "If Bob Anderson invited David Roderick and some other CEOs to form a small group, to consider real action, would Roderick respond?" "Yes," said Roderick's representative.

As a result, on June 6, 1984, at the New York headquarters of Atlantic Richfield, Anderson and Roderick met with Charles Parry, chairman of ALCOA; Louis Fernandez, then chairman of Monsanto; Louis von Planta, chairman of Ciba-Geigy; and William D. Ruckelshaus, the former head of the U.S. Environmental Protection Agency. Their purpose was to ensure that the proceedings of the WICEM conference would bear fruit. The group agreed on three key premises: that multinational corporations have much to contribute to environmental management efforts throughout the world; that multinational corporations have no less self-interest in successful environmental management than any other sector of society; and that no new organization should be created, but that a new function in the International Chamber of Commerce should be initiated to work autonomously but cooperatively inside the established ICC framework.

The IIED, meanwhile, went from strength to strength. Barbara Ward's brilliant leadership had done much to build the organization and assure its future. When she died in 1981, she was succeeded by William Clark, a former vice president of the World Bank and a distinguished publicist, who was followed in turn by Brian Walker, a former head of OXFAM, the British relief agency. Bob's enthusiasm for the cause communicated itself to others and brought in funds other than his own. ARCO had always followed his lead. When Bob gave up the chairmanship of the company in 1986, ARCO proclaimed its ongoing relationship with IIED by making a grant to it of $1 million.

Today the International Institute for Environment and Development, with its headquarters in London and operating offices in Washington and other capitals around the world, with various research programs and a steady output of information and education, is the outstanding international nongovernmental organization concerned with environmental affairs. Bob was its pioneer. Its existence and achievements are a tribute and monument to his love of nature and sense of duty to his fellow creatures.

Though he can look back with satisfaction on what he has contributed to the environmental cause, and with pride on some of the campaigns and agencies which he has pioneered if not created within it, Bob is not overly optimistic about what the future holds:

The world has experienced many golden periods, but there have been many very dark ages. Man may yet not have the wisdom, self-control and willingness to cooperate with his fellows, to prevent his own destruction by a misuse of nuclear energy. But I think that if the human race were faced with a crisis that threatened its existence, that crisis would more likely have been created by man's abuse of the environment.

Since the Stockholm conference there are a billion more people living on this planet. Another billion will have arrived by the year 2000, and another billion will arrive within fourteen years after that. To say that the presence of such numbers on this planet will not affect the environment is to ignore the facts of life. You cannot put another billion people on this planet and not feel the impact. To me the most alarming aspect of this development is that the last billion people to have arrived here are currently sustained by synthetic manufactured food. To raise that food vast amounts of various agricultural poisons, fungicides, herbicides, pesticides, together with tremendous applications of fertilizers, have to be employed. These are the ingredients which cause us most concern.

He ended his speech with a restatement of what he has always held to be the most important responsibility: the need not to fight each other, "however much fun it seems to be," and, instead, to "tread the hard path of compromise and cooperation."

We have to figure out how we can all live given the cards that we must play. The only way we can do it is to decide that we are going to find ways of working together on problems we know are not going to go away. Litigation is the last choice. Too much time has been wasted in years past by well-intentioned people working against each other. For the general good we must work together. Many of our problems have been solved, but the problems that face us become greater and greater, and the need to deal with them becomes more and more urgent. We must all pull in the same direction as never before. If that lesson has at last been learned, and will be applied, we can be hopeful that the human race will not bring about its own destruction.

CHAPTER NINE

The *Observer*, founded in 1791, and published in London on Sundays, is a British institution, regarded as one of the world's greatest newspapers. On November 24, 1976, the news broke that Bob Anderson had bought it. Nothing he has done has created more instant or widespread publicity, or so much surprise. "I was rather surprised myself," he commented blandly at the time.

The golden age of *The Observer* had begun in 1911, when it was bought by William Waldorf Astor, later the first Lord Astor, an American millionaire who domiciled himself in Britain in 1889 and became naturalized ten years later. Since he spent most of his time in Italy, his son Waldorf, husband of Nancy Astor, soon became virtual proprietor of the paper. The younger Waldorf was educated at Eton and Oxford, and went on to play a much respected role in British public life, becoming the second Lord Astor on his father's death in 1919. For the first thirty years after its purchase, *The Observer* was edited by J. L. Garvin, one of Britain's greatest journalists, a legend in his lifetime. Under Garvin the paper had on the whole supported the Conservative Party, but when he and Lord Astor parted company in 1942 *The Observer* declared in an editorial that in the future it would not be associated with a particular political party. From then on the paper behaved in the manner and spirit of the logo on its original 1791 masthead: "Unbiased by prejudice, uninfluenced by party."

In 1948 Lord Astor's second son, David, was appointed editor. Under him *The Observer* became a radical newspaper, its political stance being defined by him from time to time as "liberal with a small l." Its editorials praised or criticized the three political parties, not in general but selectively. It did not take sides at general elections. Outside politics the paper was for progress and reform. It reported and commented upon world affairs in depth and with great authority. Its book, theater and arts reviews were of the highest standard. Under David Astor, the circulation rose from about 300,000 in 1948 to a peak of more than 900,000 in 1956; the rise in sales was accompanied by a rise in the quality of its journalism.

In the early 1970s *The Observer* began to encounter difficulties. It had never sought to make money: the Astor vocation was to provide a service to the readers. Postwar inflation had undermined the paper's ability to go on doing this, and *The Observer* began to lose money. Extravagant demands for wage increases, the restrictive practices of the printing unions, the escalating cost of newsprint and the mounting competition for advertising revenue from television and radio created grave problems for all Britain's national newspapers. For *The Observer*, which had never built up any capital, and which, unlike the other two quality Sunday newspapers, *The Sunday Times* and *The Sunday Telegraph*, had no daily stable companion to subsidize it, these problems threatened to become lethal. In 1975 it was forced to lay off a third of its staff. At the end of the year, David Astor, approaching sixty-five, decided to resign after twenty-seven years as editor. He was succeeded by his thirty-eight-year-old deputy, Donald Trelford.

Eight months later the paper faced a second crisis. In spite of the measures taken in 1975, *The Observer* was still not competitive. The fall in the value of the pound had caused the cost of imported newsprint to escalate; the economic climate had gotten even worse, adversely affecting the flow of advertising revenue. The number of pages decreased, the paper looked thin, its circulation dropped to 600,000, less than two thirds of what it had been at its peak. If the paper were to survive in the long term, clearly a large injection of capital would be essential.

The Astors could not provide this. They consequently looked around for somebody who could, but who would also be willing to leave the paper alone to pursue its policy of responsible independence and high journalistic standards. David Astor and Lord Goodman, an eminent lawyer and chairman of the paper's trustees, searched for several months, but could not find anyone. By October 1976, a feeling of "near despondency," as they later put it, had settled on them.

It was then that Roger Harrison, the paper's general manager, suggested that an approach be made to Rupert Murdoch. Astor and Goodman were not happy about this. Murdoch, then negotiating the purchase of the *New York Post*, owned two papers in London, and *Observer* journalists classified them as "rags." His British mass circulation daily, *The Sun*, was famous for its page-three nudes, and his British mass-circulation Sunday, the *News of the World*, had earned him Randolph Churchill's epithet, "Pornographer Royal." Nevertheless, taking everything into account, Goodman, Astor and Harrison agreed to approach Murdoch.

He responded with interest. He would assume financial responsibility for the future of *The Observer*, he said, but he would also bring in his own editorial team and produce an *Observer* which in some respects would be different in character from what it was at the moment. Lord Goodman and Astor were in no position to demur. They now informed the editor of what was going on and arranged for him to meet Murdoch.

Despite the remarkable secrecy surrounding these events, several London newspapers reported on the morning of October 21 that *The Observer* was in the throes of a financial crisis and was about to be sold to Rupert Murdoch. *The Observer* journalists immediately held staff and union meetings to vehemently protest the idea of being taken over by Murdoch. As one journalist said, for the proprietors to sell to him was "like marrying your beautiful daughter to a gorilla." Murdoch, for his part, was angered by the leak of negotiations which he had neither sought nor initiated. He was stung by the aspersions cast upon him by *Observer* journalists. In vigorous language he called the deal off.

All this was extremely embarrassing for the proprietors of *The Observer*. In particular, the disclosure raised doubts about the paper's future, causing some agencies to switch their advertising to other publications. The only consolation was that a half-dozen other potential buyers made inquiries. The consolation was short-lived. The bidders either dropped out or proved unacceptable. Five unhappy and anxious weeks after Murdoch rejected the deal, the atmosphere within *The Observer* was one of gloom. Selling to Murdoch seemed inevitable—if, at this stage, he could be persuaded to buy it. Better Murdoch than nothing, had now become the general view.

On November 12, having come to the end of their tether, the trustees resolved to make a new approach to Murdoch in New York. Two days later, he flew to London, reportedly to clinch the deal. But by this time, unknown to more than half a dozen people on both sides of the Atlantic, Bob Anderson had intervened.

Bob's intervention came via Douglass Cater. On the day the trustees decided to make another approach to Murdoch, Cater stopped off in London for the weekend on his way to a conference in Italy. He had known for several days that *The Observer* was for sale, and on arrival was informed that this was still the case. "Perhaps Bob Anderson would be interested," he said and promptly telephoned Joe Slater. Joe at once phoned Anderson. Bob said he *would* be interested. The following day Cater went to Lord Goodman's flat, and after a brief discussion Goodman telephoned Bob in New Mexico. Twenty-four hours later David Astor, with Roger Harrison, the general manager, flew to Los Angeles. They spent a few hours with Bob and Thornton Bradshaw, and returned to London. Next day Astor received a telex which simply said: "All agreed. Go ahead and arrange deal. Anderson." Five days had elapsed since Cater's initial query.

ARCO acquired 90 percent of *The Observer*, and the former proprietors retained the rest, for the symbolic sum of one pound sterling. ARCO agreed to finance the paper from that moment on. The character and conduct of the paper, and all control of news and views to be expressed in its columns, were to be left in the hands of the editor. Before the deal was concluded, Lord Goodman put it before representatives of the staff and the unions, and it was approved. For the journalists it was a victory as well as a relief. A new board was constituted under the chairmanship of Lord Barnetson, a journalist of great repute, chairman of United Newspapers and of Reuters. Douglass Cater became vice-chairman, agreeing to spend most of the next two years in London. ARCO was directly represented by its president, Thornton Bradshaw, and by Dr. Frank Stanton, former president of the Columbia Broadcasting System. Lord Goodman and David Astor also joined the new board.

The transfer of ownership was announced on November 24, five weeks to the day after the stormy staff meetings. There was immense publicity for it both in Britain and the United States. Pictures in the papers and on television showed Bob riding on the ranch in high-heeled Mexican boots, jeans, buckskin jacket and Stetson. The British press that day carried colorful headlines: OIL KING TAKES OVER *THE OBSERVER* and THE BILLION–DOLLAR BRAIN IN A TEN-GALLON HAT. Several newspapers gave accounts of Bob's patronage of Aspen, his support of the New York theater and the Los Angeles Philharmonic Orchestra, and his work in the cause of world conservation and the environment. "His philanthropic support of learning and the arts makes one think of a rich and enlightened Renaissance prince," one paper said. The columns of *The Observer* called Bob "a latter-day Medici."

In Los Angeles Bob Anderson said, "*The Observer* is one of the world's great newspapers. It must be preserved as an independent voice in Great Britain and abroad." Thornton Bradshaw said that ARCO wanted to demonstrate that "a large American company can buy something in communications and prove by its track record that we do not influence editorial policy." In London, Lord Goodman spoke of the Aspen Institute's reputation for intellectual independence, and how this had figured in the decision of the trustees to entrust the paper to Bob Anderson.

Bob declared various motives for ARCO's acquisition of *The Observer*. Supporting this great newspaper was another reflection of

8

8

8

ARCO's policy of being a good citizen. It was a contribution to the pursuit of excellence. The possibility of acquiring *The Observer*, he said, had come up at a propitious moment. For some time ARCO had been considering taking up some activity in Europe that would give it "a window" from which Europe's, and especially Britain's, political and business developments could be observed. "You get a great deal of information from the newspapers and your business contacts abroad," he said, "but if you really want to know what's cooking in a country you need to be involved in some activity there, rubbing shoulders with the residents. We certainly hadn't thought of buying a newspaper, but when the chance came along of rescuing the world-famous *Observer*, standing for the kind of values we were already working for through the Aspen Institute, we said, 'Why not?' " He made it clear at his first talk with the proprietors that he was looking for a sensible business operation, not merely a worthy object for philanthropy. "I'm interested," he said when they discussed whether the paper could be made viable or not, "but I must be convinced that it can be done."

On the whole, the reaction to the deal was very favorable. There was some carping at the prospect of a great British newspaper becoming the property of an oil company, and some sulks that ownership of *The Observer* had passed to a citizen of another country. On both sides of the Atlantic some commentators speculated about whether Anderson had made his generous "gesture" with a view to improving his chances of acquiring licenses to drill for North Sea oil. On arrival in London for the formal conclusion of the transaction, he was interviewed extensively for TV and radio. He created a good impression and seemed to be made warmly welcome. A few days later David Astor and Lord Goodman gave a grand dinner for him in London, attended by one hundred fifty "eminent luminaries of public life," including five members of the Cabinet, leading members of the Opposition, six newspaper "barons," and men eminent in the fields of culture, law, medicine, literature, learning and the arts. This glittering occasion, according to one reporter, enabled Bob Anderson to "sample his first taste of the power and the glory peculiar to the ownership of one of the world's most renowned newspapers."

* * *

Bob's four-year ownership of *The Observer* much influenced the future of the paper, and his stewardship of it influenced the British perception of him. *The Observer*, inevitably, was a stage on which he could not escape being seen. The relationships between Bob Anderson and his colleagues on the one hand, and Lord Goodman and David Astor on the other, were happy and fruitful. When at the end of the first twelve months Lord Goodman and Astor recommended that the distinguished Irish politician, diplomat and writer, Dr. Conor Cruise O'Brien, be appointed editor in chief, Bob accepted their recommendation without discussion. O'Brien remained in that post for about three years. Over the four-year period of its stewardship ARCO spent about $16 million on the paper. Though the increase in its circulation was marginal, it was clear that its potential had been much improved. It had been promoted to a degree that had not been possible in the years prior to ARCO's taking over. Its advertising revenue was increasing, not diminishing. Carrying more pages, it was becoming a more attractive product. Much had been spent in upgrading the building and its facilities. ARCO had done *The Observer* proud. They had cherished its editorial independence and had invested large sums in maintaining its character and quality. Lord Goodman described ARCO as "a model newspaper proprietor."

The downside of the relationship, from Bob Anderson's point of view, was that *The Observer* showed no sign at all of being able to exist without ARCO's increasingly large annual subsidy. This was a serious matter. Bob had committed ARCO to support of *The Observer*, believing on the basis of what he had been told—in all good faith—that the paper's losses in the first few years would not be large and that in due course it could be made profitable. He had said as much at the time to those ARCO directors who had intimated misgivings about the acquisition, and continued to express them. As the years went by, his attention was more frequently drawn to the fact that the paper showed no signs of making money; on the contrary, the deficit was increasing yearly.

Though the galloping rate of inflation in the later 1970s was an important factor, the main element in the annual deficit was the losses resulting from strikes or industrial disputes. Most of these stoppages were unofficial, disapproved of by the national leaders of the printing unions, launched on a Saturday sometimes at a few minutes' notice, and led by some of the most militant local union leaders in the country, motivated, it was alleged, as much politically as financially. It was no comfort to *The Observer* that most other newspapers suffered, too: Sunday newspapers with daily stable companions, and dailies on sale six times a week, were in an altogether less vulnerable position.

In the fall of 1980, a protracted unofficial industrial dispute at *The Observer*, launched by a handful of militants, was terminated only after the British management had threatened to close the paper down if the terms approved by the union's official leaders were not accepted. Bob became worried: the possibility loomed that an American company might be held responsible for the extinction of a great British newspaper, the newspaper it had come into the country to rescue. That unofficial dispute was the main factor in ARCO's having to meet a deficit that year of about $6 million.

Later that fall, Lord Barnetson resigned as chairman. He was succeeded by Thornton Bradshaw, but Bradshaw, about to leave ARCO and become chairman of RCA, soon resigned as well. Douglass Cater, temporarily removed from London in the first instance by the necessity for a heart operation, had long since returned permanently to the United States to open up new ground for the Aspen Institute. Reluctantly, since he was busy on many other fronts, Bob decided to take on the chairmanship himself.

Two board meetings sufficed to bring him face-to-face with the fundamental question: how could a sound economic base be constructed for *The Observer*, given the attitude of the unions and the fact that the proprietors were foreigners who lived nearly six thousand miles away? At his first meeting with David Astor four years previously he had said he was looking for "a sensible business operation." In view of the behavior of the unions, and its foreign ownership, would the paper *ever* become a sensible business operation? He had always said that if the task proved too difficult, in *The Observer*'s own interest the relationship with ARCO should be terminated.

In the first few weeks of 1981 Bob began to consider the situation in earnest. An *Observer* board meeting was held on Friday, February 20, 1981. Nothing he heard around the table suggested to him that the financial situation of the paper had improved, or that it was likely to improve in the foreseeable future. A change in the attitude of the unions looked most unlikely. It seemed that the only thing that could be relied upon to end an official strike was a threat to close the paper down.

Before Bob flew back to Los Angeles the following Sunday, he had a meeting with the CEO of Lonrho Ltd., Roland ("Tiny") Rowland. Lonrho, a multinational conglomerate based in London, was engaged in a wide range of activities from mining to distilling whisky. It owned several newspapers in Africa and three in Scotland. Bob was on friendly terms with Rowland. He knew that Tiny was keen to acquire a quality national newspaper, and that he was particularly interested in *The Observer* since its reputation was high in Africa, where Lonrho had many interests. Mr. Rowland now proposed a deal. Bob Anderson decided to sell *The Observer* to him.

The deal was announced simultaneously in Los Angeles and London the following Wednesday. Bob did not consult his fellow directors on *The Observer* board beforehand, or let them know what he had decided to do. He did not take the editor into his confidence. He remembered how hard Lord Goodman and David Astor had tried to keep secret their original negotiations with Rupert Murdoch in 1976. Recalling the various kinds of damage done to the paper between the first Murdoch offer and its acquisition by ARCO, he feared that if he communicated his thoughts to the board, anything he said would become public and inevitably cause damaging speculation about the paper's future.

When the deal was announced, Bob was criticized for keeping his colleagues in the dark about his intention to sell. Journalists complained that newspapers should not be transferred from one owner to another without previous consultation with the staff. Lord Goodman and David Astor felt hurt not only because they had not been consulted about a change of ownership, but also because they had rejected Rowland as a purchaser some years previously.

Trouble was in store. When Bob and Tiny agreed to deal, they knew that under the 1973 Fair Trading Act the transfer of ownership would have to be approved by the secretary of state for trade and industry. Under the act, the department was required to forbid any transaction which would give a businessman an unfair advantage over his competitors, and if it considered such an unfair advantage might arise it was required to "refer" the proposed transaction to the Monopolies Commission and obtain from it a report and a recommendation. This procedure had not been set in motion when ARCO acquired the paper, on the grounds that ARCO did not own any other British newspaper; permission for the sale was given immediately. Lonrho's position was different; they already owned some newspapers in Scotland. Though these were not nationwide newspapers, and their circulation figures were modest, there was the possibility that if a new acquisition were added to these, Lonrho would gain an unfair trading advantage over their competitors, at any rate in Scotland.

Bob and Tiny were confident that Secretary of State John Biffen would consent to the transfer without referring it to the commission. They based this sanguine view on the fact that only a few weeks before, when Rupert Murdoch, who already owned two national newspapers, asked permission to buy a third, *The Times*, the Department of Trade "nodded" his application through. They thought the same thing would happen to the sale of *The Observer*.

They were wrong. Sharply criticized in the House of Commons for his "nod" toward Murdoch, Biffen now deemed it prudent to refer *The Observer* deal to the commission. For Bob and Tiny it was a blow. They knew the commission would take at least several weeks to complete its report: one object of Bob's swiftness and secrecy in arranging the deal had already been defeated.

When Biffen decided not to "nod" *The Observer* deal through, he mainly had in mind the need to ensure that if it did go through it would not give Rowland an unfair trading advantage over his competitors. But once he had "referred" it, it became clear that most of the commission's time would be taken up in listening to people claiming that the deal would operate against "the need for the free expression of news and views," which was a second condition the 1973 Fair Trading Act was intended to secure. The critics of the deal drew attention to the fact that Rowland had vast business interests in Africa and the United Kingdom. They alleged that he would use *The Observer*'s columns to further these interests, and would suppress news and views which might damage them. Even if he did not actively interfere, they alleged, the editor and staff—being aware of the proprietor's interests—would be inhibited in what they reported and in the opinions they expressed. The famous independence of *The Observer* would be compromised.

Between March and June the commission held twenty-one hearings. In the two appearances he was asked to make, Bob impressed its members with his candid account of ARCO's "stewardship" of *The Observer*, and of how he had come to the conclusion it was in the best interests of the paper to be owned and managed by a British company with newspaper experience, rather than by an American oil firm located six thousand miles away. The commission asked him whether in the event the deal went through he was prepared to remain chairman of *The Observer*. He replied that he would be glad to do so, if that was the general wish. Rowland and his colleagues were naturally asked to make several appearances before the commission. The editor of *The Observer*, its two joint managing directors and several senior members of its staff also made submissions.

Some of those who testified were strongly opposed to Rowland's acquisition of the paper and expressed considerable criticism of him. Some of them made statements to the press, which they were entitled to do if they wished, and some lobbied members of Parliament to make representations to the commission. There was a great deal of correspondence in the letters column of *The Times*. The feelings of some partisans ran high. Rumors were often repeated as though they were fact. The four months which passed between the announcement of the deal and Secretary of State Biffen's decision to approve it were not easy for those involved.

The commission completed its report in June 1981, concluding that, providing some undertakings were given, the deal was acceptable. In early July, Biffen gave his consent to the transfer of ownership. Murdoch had been allowed to purchase *The Times* on condition that a number of independent directors be appointed with power to protect the editor from any attempt which the owner might make to influence the paper's editorial content. The secretary of state followed that precedent in the case of *The Observer*, with the result that there are now five directors on its board with the power to deal with any complaint made to them by the editor about the owner, to approve or prevent any move to fire him and to veto the appointment of his successor. The editor of *The Observer* is the most protected editor on Fleet Street.

The deal put *The Observer* into Lonrho's newspaper subsidiary, George Outram and Company, but left it free to run itself as before. ARCO acquired a 20 percent share of Outram and $4.5 million in cash. Bob Anderson continued as chairman of *The Observer* and Tiny Rowland became his deputy. He remained chairman for three years, then stepped down in favor of Rowland.

Today Lonrho is sole owner of *The Observer*. The editor has frequently written and spoken in public about the editorial independence he enjoys. The paper's journalistic quality is higher today than it has been for twenty years, and in the last several years it has won an unprecedented number of awards for the excellence of its writing and of its design. Its circulation is about 15 percent higher than it was when ARCO acquired it. It is making a good profit. Looking back, Bob says, "On balance we neither made nor lost any significant amount of money—which is something of a success story for Fleet Street today."

CHAPTER TEN

In 1982 Bob pulled off what may well turn out to be the biggest deal of his—and ARCO's—life, a coup with great consequences for the United States and the Western world as a whole. He signed a contract with the government of China which allowed ARCO to drill for oil offshore. The undertaking was put in the hands of Paul Ravesies, president of ARCO's International Oil and Gas Company.

ARCO International Oil and Gas is Atlantic Richfield's division in charge of exploring, developing and producing oil and gas outside the United States. Ravesies has great freedom. He handles ARCO's North Sea oil investments and operations, its interests in Africa, South America, Southeast Asia and now China. Usually his group does the research and then presents a project to senior management for discussion with Bob Anderson. One of the most important functions of Ravesies's operations is the cataloguing and updating of a record of potentially useful information about every part of the world outside the United States. "At any time," said Ravesies, "there is a list of countries we *would* go into and a list of countries we *wouldn't* go into." In the case of China, however, the initiative came from Bob. It all started with Bob Anderson going to Beijing in the summer of 1978, a visit he made not in connection with ARCO, but as chairman of a delegation organized by the Aspen Institute. Before Bob left for

155

Beijing, Ravesies pressed upon him a little book which contained information about what projects ARCO might be interested in pursuing in China if they got the chance.

In Beijing, there were a number of meetings with high-ranking members of the Chinese government. One of these was Vice Premier Li Xiannian. Bob and General Li got on very well. They had a long talk about China's needs and how the United States could help. It was important for China to develop its resources of oil, natural gas and coal, said the general, and to do this effectively and quickly it would be necessary to cooperate in joint ventures with industrial firms from outside the country. Foreign enterprises would not be welcome on the mainland, but China had great resources offshore. Bob said that ARCO would be glad to help. General Li seemed amenable. When Bob got back to Los Angeles he talked at length to Ravesies about what should be the next move. Ravesies drafted a cable to General Li in Bob's name asking if Li would talk to Ravesies if he went to Beijing. Several weeks went by in silence. A doubting Thomas told Ravesies he "might as well have thrown that cable out of the window." Bob remained sanguine. "Say, Paul," he said, "why don't you turn it around and invite *them* to come over and see *us*? Tell them you'll send our 707 over for them, suggest they bring fifteen or twenty over, tell them you'll show them all our operations in the States, take them around to do some sightseeing and give them a dinner in Washington, D.C." Ravesies sent the invitation worded along those lines, adding on his own initiative an offer to take them to Disneyland.

The invitation was accepted. ("I reckon it was Disneyland that did it," said Bob.) The only reservation the Chinese made was that the ARCO plane should not come to the mainland but should pick them up in Tokyo. A few weeks later three ARCO executives from the International Oil and Gas Company met the Chinese party in Tokyo and flew them to Washington where they could visit their embassy. From there the Chinese were flown to see ARCO's operations in oil, gas, minerals, and fertilizers, as well as work on solar energy equipment. They were flown to Alaska, and visited Anchorage, the North Slope and Prudhoe Bay. When they arrived in Los Angeles, ARCO executives invited the Chinese to their homes. Ravesies has a collection of photographs of the Chinese visitors standing outside various ARCO plants, and in front of sundry places of historical interest, including Disneyland. "They really liked that," he said. "It was the high point of their trip."

Shortly thereafter, ARCO was invited to send a delegation to China. Discussions with the minister of fuel began at once, with officials from the Ministry of Foreign Affairs and of other participating departments. For the next two weeks—"The Chinese don't bother about Sundays; you work right through," said Ravesies—the two teams sat facing each other across broad desks talking from eight in the morning until noon and then from half-past one until six in the evening. The broad basis of a contract began to emerge. The Chinese wanted ARCO to finance the exploration, jointly develop and produce, and, then, in the words of Ravesies, "turn over the operation to the Chinese, all greased up and going, in exchange for a share of the profits if and when profits were forthcoming." They also wanted ARCO to train a sufficient number of Chinese to manage operations when ARCO withdrew.

ARCO gladly accepted these terms. From the point of view of the company, the shareholders stood to benefit from the hoped-for discovery of substantial amounts of oil or gas, or both; and ARCO, having been the first to do business with the Chinese, would have a considerable edge over any potential competitors when other deals came along. From the point of view of the American people, ARCO thought, the deal showed that a capitalist country could work with a Communist country to mutual benefit: a contribution to the dialogue between East and West which, in ARCO's view, was essential to the preservation of world peace and the reduction of world poverty.

So the ARCO team, tired but happy, returned to Los Angeles, having undertaken to send back a comprehensive legal contract in thirty days. They worked day and night with the ARCO lawyers. On the twenty-eighth day a 150-page draft went to the Chinese government. "There were a great many difficulties," said Ravesies. "For instance, the Chinese had no tax laws—they had to invent some to make this deal work. Another thing: they don't have what we call lawyers; they have 'advisors,' and they take an awfully long time over everything because they don't have a body of rules and regulations to apply to whatever you suggest—they have to look at every detail on its own merits." There were a number of exchanges. The Chinese were slow, cautious and nervous, and asked many questions. It was a full year before the terms of the contract were concluded in the autumn of 1981. A date was fixed for Bob to go over and sign it— January 1, 1982. Then, just before Christmas, the Chinese said they wished to postpone the signing—more queries had come up. For how long did they wish to postpone the consummation? They were not able to say; they wished to postpone until further notice. There was anxious speculation in Los Angeles. Were the Chinese backing out?

Finally, seven days later, a list of queries arrived from China—and "they were very reasonable ones," commented Ravesies. A few months later the terms were completed. "Actually, the Chinese behaved very well," said Ravesies. "The only real trouble was they moved so slowly. But after all, this was new to them. They'd never done this kind of thing before. From start to finish they were completely straight and aboveboard. And very courteous." On September 15, 1982, the 707 took off from Los Angeles carrying Bob and six top ARCO executives. This time they were invited to land in Beijing.

An observer accompanying the ARCO party throughout the four-day trip would have had the impression of being with a mission that had arrived to sign an international treaty. The Americans landed at ten o'clock at night and were taken to the VIP lounge to be greeted by the minister of energy, a representative of the Foreign Office and a group of officials. They were then driven to a governmental guest-house standing in a beautiful park about five miles from the center of the capital. Over the next four days there were several meetings with ministers and officials from several different government departments: Bob and the senior minister present sat side by side in easy chairs at the far end, an interpreter between them, and the rest of the ARCO men sat down the length of the room on Bob's right, and along the opposite side of the room sat the Chinese. In front of each armchair was a small table on which were a drinking dish and a teapot, which was replenished from time to time by young ladies carrying kettles. Since by now the terms of the contract had been worked over with a fine-tooth comb, the conversation essentially consisted of compliments, expressions of goodwill and observations on the relations between the two countries. These sessions lasted for about ninety minutes. The atmosphere was extremely cordial, and the Chinese made a great many jokes, including the familiar one, "It is for you capitalists to take the risks. *We* are socialists."

The ceremony of the signing took place on the morning of September 19, 1982, in an enormous chamber in the Great Hall of the People, which stands in the Gate of Heavenly Peace Square, in the heart of Beijing, where the establishment of the People's Republic was proclaimed in September 1949. Nearly four years had elapsed since Bob Anderson had had his first conversations with General Li, and the contract had taken more than three years to negotiate. Under the agreement, ARCO was to have a 70 percent interest in a 2.2 million acre block—the Yingge Hai block, located sixty-five miles south of the island of Hainan in the South China Sea, about two hundred miles east of the coast of Vietnam. ARCO's junior partner, Santa Fe Minerals, was to have a 30 percent interest. ARCO would do the drilling and operate the discovered fields, cooperating with the Chinese government through the Chinese National Offshore Oil Corporation (CNOOC).

On this occasion, it was the vice premier in charge of foreign affairs who sat alongside Bob at the top of the room. After compliments had been exchanged and two rounds of tea had been drunk, the vice premier began to ask Bob for advice in other fields—transport, chemicals, fertilizers, solar energy and minerals, particularly coal. At the end of the session the two principals shook hands, and Bob, with the cameras flashing, promised that ARCO would give any help it could. The meeting ended in an atmosphere of great good humor, hope and mutual trust.

Three months went by before drilling could begin. A drilling ship had to make its slow way across the Pacific to the offshore site, and a twenty-eight-man ARCO team had to be flown to China to establish an operations headquarters at Zhenjiang on the mainland. The early months were frustrating: much of the work done by ARCO's staff in

China would have been better done in the ARCO laboratories in Los Angeles, but the Chinese would allow nothing to be taken out of China which might yield valuable data to foreigners. After many months of patient explanation, however, ARCO persuaded the Chinese government to allow geophysical and seismic data to be flown to Los Angeles for interpretation, but only on condition that seven Chinese technicians accompany the data to look over the ARCO men's shoulders.

The drilling ship, the *Glomar Java Sea 2*, began work in January 1983. The first well turned out to be a dry hole. The ship was moved twenty miles to the south, and this time a large accumulation of gas was discovered. To obtain more information about the size and nature of this field, the rig was sailed to another location. Here, on the morning of October 26, a disaster occurred. This area of the South China Sea is subject to typhoons, and one of them hit the *Glomar Java Sea 2*, sinking it and causing the loss of all eighty-one aboard. The following April, confident that the newly discovered gas field was going to prove a great success, ARCO hired another drilling ship, *Fluor 9*, and a brand-new semi-submersible rig made in Japan, the *Zapata Arctic*, and resumed drilling. On August 14, 1984, Paul Ravesies was able to announce in Los Angeles that final testing of the Yingge Hai location had confirmed a potential production capacity of several hundred million cubic feet of gas per day. This was a giant field. There was great rejoicing in Beijing and Los Angeles.

The question now was how to use the gas. The previous December, Bob and Paul had flown to Beijing for a talk with the great Deng Xiaoping himself. Bob told Deng that ARCO had been looking at a number of possibilities. "I told him that we had considered liquefying it, making methanol out of it, or generating electrical power with it. We'd even gone into the possibility of constructing a pipeline from Hainan to Hong Kong, then on up to Guangzhou [Canton] and generating the power up there. But particularly since China's greatest need was for fertilizer—at that time the Chinese were importing seven million tons of it a year at great cost—the best thing to do with the gas was to take it to Hainan island by pipeline, which we knew how to build, build the necessary plant and convert the gas into urea, which is used in the manufacture of fertilizer. The plant, I told him, would supply a large percentage of China's needs. Deng was very impressed."

When Bob got back to Los Angeles the ARCO fertilizer experts began work on designs for a plant. The latest reports from Yingge Hai indicated that enough urea could be manufactured to make China self-sufficient in fertilizer. In April Bob flew back to Beijing with two large-scale models, which he presented to Deng ceremoniously in the Great Hall of the People. By the time the existence of the giant field was confirmed in August, Bob and Deng were considering three possibilities: building a huge ammonia plant which would produce urea; the same, to produce ammonia; and in either case, using any excess gas to generate power for Hainan island. The cost of this massive undertaking, they estimated, would be about $4 billion. They agreed to hold further meetings in September and October and aim for a final decision on how to use the gas in mid-November. Meanwhile the Chinese began to talk about involving one or more European countries in the vast operation, particularly the United Kingdom, whose success in exploiting North Sea gas had very much impressed them.

Time went by. There were some newspaper reports that ARCO's find was in waters belonging to Vietnam; a congressional committee asked Paul Ravesies about this, and he was able to assure them that the field was at least sixty-five miles outside Vietnamese waters. ARCO's rigs drilled other wells: some turned out to be dry, others not big enough to be worth developing. Transport, labor, communications and services posed many problems for the ARCO staff at Zhenjiang: their water supply did not function until eleven o'clock at night and went off at one o'clock in the morning, but it was clear that the Chinese were working increasingly hard to help solve them.

In August 1985, ARCO was able to tell the world that it was about to develop a field now classified as a "super giant." It was clear to all that ARCO was the first company in the world to register a significant success in China. ARCO would shortly begin to operate the field, and build a drilling and production platform, the first to be constructed by an American company off the shore of China. ARCO also announced details of the building of the sixty-five-mile pipeline from the field to the island. Bob flew to Beijing, and on September 28 signed another agreement in the Great Hall of the People.

The terms of this agreement, however, were different in one very important respect from those which had been discussed for many months after the Yingge Hai field was discovered. By now, after considerable discussion with ARCO, the Chinese had changed their mind about how the gas was to be used: instead of using it mainly for the manufacture of urea they now intended to use it for the generation of electric power. Though a small amount of the gas would be converted into urea, the project for the fertilizer plant on Hainan island was abandoned. Instead, the Chinese agreed to spend a large proportion of an estimated $400 million to finance an equally ambitious project: a production platform and subsea pipeline which would take the gas from the Yingge Hai field to Hainan island at the rate of 350 million cubic feet per day. They would spend several billion dollars more to build an undersea pipeline complex to Guangzhou on the mainland and an overland distribution network to supply power plants and other customers in Guangzhou, Shenzhen and Hong Kong. The benefits for Guangzhou and the surrounding economic zone would be immense. When Bob signed the agreement, Guangzhou was desperately short of energy: some of its factories, it was reported, were working only half days. Other cities were also said to be in difficulties.

So far, ARCO has made the only major discovery in the South China Sea. The most recent reports indicate that the field is bigger than was estimated six months ago and that it can probably deliver a billion cubic feet of gas a day, the equivalent of 166,000 barrels of oil a day. The pipeline to take the oil from Hainan to Guangzhou and Hong Kong is currently being designed. The Yingge Hai field is being delineated, and a production platform could be in place by the end of summer 1988. If this schedule is followed the pipeline will be in use by 1989.

ARCO has also looked at coal in China. The subject of coal came up when Bob sat chatting with the vice premier just after the signing of the 1982 contract. "We can help you find the coal," said Bob. "We can help you extract it, and we can help you bring it down to where you want it." ARCO was invited to operate the Shen Mu coal field north of Beijing, one of China's most promising coal-producing areas, in Bob's view; a railroad would be built to bring the loads down to the cities. Given the problems posed by the rough mountain terrain, constructing the railway would be a world-scale project. Between 20 and 30 million tons of coal would be mined a year. The Chinese planned to use the coal in China instead of the fuel oil, so that fuel oil would be available for export where it would earn them hard currency in the world market. After much study, however, ARCO decided to give up this opportunity.

ARCO originally went to China to try to find oil rather than gas or coal. So far it has found no oil in China, though it has found more energy in the form of gas than any other company in the world has, but hopes are higher than ever. Bob also initiated negotiations with the Chinese government for permission to drill in the very remote Tarim Basin, which lies immediately to the north of Tibet and to the south of Outer Mongolia, on the edge of the old silk route from Europe to Beijing. "I have a hunch that this area is going to be very rich in oil, and that Tarim Basin will be a great oil province," said Bob. "This will be the last great hurrah for the oil industry. I don't think there's another area in the world which has the same potential. If we find oil it will take three thousand miles of pipeline to bring it to navigable waters. It'll be a hell of a challenge. It's total desert, high altitude, with enormous sand dunes and virtually impassable. The geological party will have to be able to move great distances sustaining itself on its own resources. We'd have to operate far away from the nearest human settlements. We'd have to build our own base and provide our own camps. But if we can find oil in Alaska and build a pipeline to bring it out, I see no reason why we won't be able to do the same in China, though, of course, it'll take longer; it's unlikely any oil will move out of there this century. But you've got to look ahead. It would be a great day for China if we found oil there, and I want ARCO to be the ones to do it."

CHAPTER ELEVEN

On the morning of Tuesday, May 4, 1982, several months before ARCO signed the contract with the Chinese, Bob, now sixty-five years old, rose to his feet in the Beverly Wilshire Hotel in Los Angeles and opened the eighteenth annual Atlantic Richfield stockholders' meeting. He had done this seventeen times before, but this year there was a difference: he announced his resignation as chief executive officer. He had passed the statutory age limit in April. He would remain chairman of the company, but William F. Kieschnick, then president and chief operating officer, would succeed him as CEO. Sitting close to Bob as he spoke was Thornton Bradshaw, still on the ARCO board, and now the successful chairman and CEO of RCA as well. Theirs had been a remarkable partnership.

To most of those present at the stockholders' meeting, ARCO's future had never looked brighter. The price of a barrel of oil had never been so high. Exploration and development were proceeding at a most gratifying pace. More oil and gas was expected from the North Sea field. Supplies and reserves on the North Slope had exceeded the most sanguine hopes. The prospects for the China contract were rosy. The American economy seemed in pretty good shape.

ARCO itself looked in pretty good shape, at any rate to the great majority of its beholders. It was now the tenth largest industrial corporation in the United States and the twelfth largest in the world.

At this time, it was made up of eleven entities. ARCO Exploration Company and ARCO Oil and Gas Company, both with headquarters in Dallas, explored and produced respectively in North America; the ARCO International Oil and Gas Company did the same abroad. ARCO Petroleum Products manufactured and distributed fuels. The Transportation Company managed and operated pipelines and tankers. The ARCO Chemical Company, based in Philadelphia, manufactured and sold commodity petrochemicals and specialty chemicals. There were three Anaconda companies: the Copper Company handled the exploration and distribution of copper and other non-hydrocarbon minerals; the Anaconda Industries Company manufactured and sold various electronics equipment and metal products; and the Aluminum Company mined, refined, fabricated and sold primary aluminum and aluminum products around the world. The ARCO Coal Company, based in Denver, explored for and sold coal in the U.S. and Australia. Finally, the newest, and in some respects the most exciting, company was ARCO Ventures. Its main interest was in solar energy, but it operated a number of companies manufacturing and selling solar collectors, heating and cooling equipment, and it conducted solar energy research. ARCO Ventures also developed new opportunities in high-technology areas relating to the environment, energy and agriculture. It produced its own seeds. Asked what ARCO Ventures did, Bob once replied, "They are growing tomorrow's new industries."

This was a vast enterprise, by any standard. During the previous financial year, its earnings had reached $1.7 billion on revenues of $28.2 billion and assets of $19.7 billion. There were more than 200,000 shareholders. Bob had come a long way from his third share in a little refinery in Artesia.

The outlook for ARCO was splendid on the day Bob resigned as chief executive, but when he gave up the chairmanship three years later, things looked different. Much had happened in those years to both the American and global economies, to the oil industry and to ARCO.

ARCO's fortunes had sustained a blow two years earlier, when the collapse of the world copper market had forced it to suspend the non–

coal mining operations of its Anaconda division. Then, in 1984, Bob failed for the first time to acquire a company he had set out to buy—Gulf Oil. He was, as he put it, "beaten in the straight" by Chevron, which offered more. It turned out to be a blessing in disguise. The following year came the slump in oil prices. Chevron had done ARCO a favor.

By now, it was clear that the world recession and the adverse conditions it had created for the oil industry were not going to pass in a year or two. When he became chief executive in 1982, Kieschnick had begun to slim ARCO's non-oil operations and get rid of unprofitable or low-return activities. The decline in oil prices from $42 in 1980 to $29 in 1983 had made this housecleaning imperative.

In the fall of 1984, crude oil prices weakened again. This was especially alarming because crude oil prices should have been strengthening with the higher demand required by winter. Bob, working with Bill Kieschnick and ARCO management, concluded that the OPEC cartel was not going to perform as expected. The interests of its members were in conflict. Too many OPEC countries were trying to take advantage of Saudi Arabia, and the Saudis were going to retaliate.

The new ARCO crude oil price forecast was $18 a barrel, an astoundingly low forecast at that time. Internal management and the outside world were to be shocked by the forecast and its consequences. All past investment bets were off.

Bob pushed hard to bring domestic exploration spending under control. Given the situation, domestic exploration was simply too expensive. Besides, Bob noted, ARCO could buy its own stock. This gave its shareholders reserves at a bargain price compared to the cost of its own domestic exploration efforts. Kieschnick reluctantly decided to cut the domestic exploration program. Bob agreed with Kieschnick that ARCO could not afford to wait for the world minerals market to recover: all minerals operations, except for coal, had to go. They agreed that the future of ARCO's oil and gas production lay with international operations, together with Alaska. Growth in international production would continue. As part of its sweeping new program ARCO would sell or shut down all of its 1,350 filling stations east of the Mississippi, and sell the Philadelphia refinery. Its work force of 54,000 would be reduced by nearly half over the next three years.

This basic program having been agreed upon, it was essential to carry it out with all possible speed and secrecy. Only a handful of executives were made privy to it, and they worked day and night to map out the details. The cutbacks would be accompanied by an audacious $4-billion buy-in of the company stock. Until this could be announced publicly, nothing of it was to leak out. Before the announcement could be made, the necessary legal papers would have to be prepared for, and approved by, the ARCO board, and the Securities and Exchange Commission filings signed. Moreover, ARCO, always concerned about its treatment of its employees, wanted a special severance plan in place, and to have its senior management informed and ready to explain what was happening to employees, and to the press, on the day of the announcement. Bob's deadline for the completion of this schedule put a strain on the small circle of ARCO executives involved, supplemented with a select few investment bankers, public accountants and lawyers. On April 10, Bob decided that they had it right. He then informed the members of the ARCO board that there would be a secret meeting on Sunday, April 28, in the company's Anaconda Tower in Denver.

The day before the Sunday board meeting in Denver, the ARCO air fleet brought thirty senior managers from different parts of the country into ARCO's headquarters in Los Angeles. They were thoroughly briefed on what was about to happen, and their tasks for Monday were outlined. The fleet then whisked them back to their homes, and, having set them down, immediately took off to collect the members of the board and bring them to Denver. When they assembled in the Anaconda Tower, they were informed that there had been a crucial reassessment of the future of crude oil prices, and that the new assumptions required a new ARCO.

The board deliberated for six hours, and concurred. The SEC filings were signed and dispatched to New York in a company jet. Press statements were to be released one hour before the New York Stock Exchange opened for trading on Monday. Demand for ARCO stock poured in at such a rate that the stock exchange specialist could not open the stock for another hour. Its price jumped from $48 to varying figures in the sixties; ARCO's market value went up by an astonishing $3 billion. Bob and ARCO had turned adversity into a triumph.

He told a press conference: "Our plans will emphasize our strong reserve position as a net producer of crude oil and natural gas. Our company has always emphasized entrepreneurial action and the ability to react to opportunity and changed circumstance. This has built tremendous values for our shareholders. This program evidences our determination to maintain that realistic style."

A few months later, in December 1985, the Saudis launched their crude oil price war. ARCO's forecast had been correct.

Two months after the April board meeting in Denver, Kieschnick, who had only two years to go as chief executive, made way for Lod Cook, five years younger, who had enough years ahead of him to be able to see the enormous new program through.

By the end of 1985 it was clear to Bob that Lod Cook, after three months as chief executive, had his hands firmly on the company's reins and was carrying out the program with all due speed. This was the time, he decided, to display his complete confidence in Lod, and his faith in the future of ARCO, by stepping down from the chairmanship. In spite of Lod's request that he remain chairman for two more years, which would take him to the age of seventy, he announced his resignation the following January.

Bob, nonetheless, remained chairman of the executive committee. "Bob Anderson retires," commented the ARCO *Spark*, "but don't go offering him any rocking chair." Though he was giving up the chairmanship he was not giving up ARCO. "I don't see myself as retiring, but more as just changing jobs. As a matter of fact, I'll be going back to the job I had originally as chairman of the executive committee. And I expect to be an active director. I certainly don't see myself as a rocking-chair retiree."

He pointed out that in "this period of uncertainty for the oil industry," one thing in particular would happen: "The domestic oil industry, in particular, is beginning to feel the adverse effects that all of American industry has faced. There's obviously a shift to more international activities."

The 1986 stockholders' meeting was the first Bob had not chaired for twenty years. Oil was $14 a barrel, exactly half its price at the time of the stockholders' meeting a year before. Lod Cook was not pessimistic despite the price of oil. "The good news," he said, "is that your management, under the leadership of Bob Anderson and Bill Kieschnick, laid the foundation to meet this difficult environment." The claim was borne out by the year's first-quarter figures: they were strong, and earnings per share were $1.58, compared to $1.47 the previous year.

Lod paid tribute to Bob Anderson's contributions to the development of ARCO: "In many respects he is the founder of the company." ARCO President Bob Wycoff followed him with a report of the activities of the various ARCO companies, and a review of the reshaped, slimmed and reorganized corporation as a whole. "I think you can see that we are a very different company from the past," he concluded. "To underline that fact, we've decided to make an image change related to the name of our company. The names linked by the 1966 merger—Atlantic and Richfield—have long held distinguished places in the American petroleum industry. They go back to the roots of this business. Yet ever since the two companies were joined, we have become more and more familiar as, simply, ARCO. And that's the name we'll be presenting to the public henceforth."

Bob Wycoff was right. ARCO had now become "a very different company." Over a period of nearly a quarter of a century Bob had put together a great collection of industrial entities of diverse characters, and even before he resigned as chief executive officer in 1982 the time had clearly come for ARCO to take stock of itself, prune, regroup, consolidate and reorganize. The decline in the world market for oil made the task urgent and essential. "We were lucky that Bob was here when we had to face it," said Lod Cook. "There is nobody in the world who has known the oil business as he has. His experience is unique."

In view of that "unique" knowledge of the oil business, Bob's views of its and ARCO's future are frequently solicited. The first thing he mentions usually is the need to shift from domestic to international operations. "ARCO is extremely fortunate to have resources almost unmatched by any other American oil company. Yet despite our strong domestic crude position, we face an environment in which we must shift increasingly toward international operations. In the past, foreign earnings were a less significant part of our earnings. That will change." One of the most important factors bringing about this change is the American tax structure. "The way this affects exploration of domestic oil and gas is a considerable disincentive." He believes the future of the company will lie in its foreign operations. "More and more of our employees will be foreign nationals or young Americans working abroad for a substantial period of their careers." Many of them, he believes, may be working in China. "There will be further development of China's resources, one of the last great markets and perhaps one of the last great oil and gas reserves. ARCO's oil and gas discovery in China compares favorably with our finds in the United States."

He considers that some of ARCO's businesses other than oil and gas have great potential in foreign markets. "ARCO's Solar Inc.'s greatest opportunities already lie outside the United States, in countries where there is plenty of sun and where remote sources of energy are needed. And ARCO Chemical is so technologically advanced it will have an edge in many foreign petrochemical markets."

As to the future of ARCO as a company: "We have great strength; most of ARCO's intrinsic value is represented by its underground and future reserves, and it's these which constitute the underpinning of a successful operator. As a result of our restructuring we are a much stronger and more competitive company than we were before."

For three months after the 1986 general meeting there seemed to be little change in the pattern of Bob Anderson's life. His commitments and his pursuits did not differ much from what they had been before. He had never spent much time at his desk in Los Angeles, and for three months he continued to spend no less time in the office than he did when he was chairman. He made much the same number of visits to Washington, New York, Chicago and Denver as he had always made. As before there were frequent trips to the various headquarters of the Aspen Institute. Most Fridays he headed for the ranch on the Hondo, to ride, fish and hunt, have dinner at the Silver Dollar with one or both of his sons and their wives, and be with any of the eighteen grandchildren who were visiting. Back to Los Angeles after lunch on Sunday, and to the ARCO office on Monday. He frequently took a trip to London, Istanbul, Moscow or Beijing. It was very much the same mixture as before. Far from taking to a rocking chair, he had hardly changed his way of life.

Just how far he was from his rocking chair became clear in August. To the immense surprise of most people in the oil world, it was announced that Robert O. Anderson had resigned from the board of ARCO. He remarked on this decision: "Everything has come to an end. It struck me that this was a suitable moment for me to terminate my official connection with ARCO. The company is in great shape. It is in a splendid position to take advantage of what has been accomplished in the last two years. The outlook for petroleum, it has now become clear, is improving, and the future of ARCO looks extremely promising. Its leadership is in safe hands.

"This, therefore, is a time when I feel free to gratify an urge which has been gnawing at me for several years past—to return to the freedom and the excitement of being an independent oil and gas operator. Most people today think of me as the head, and creator, of a great oil company, but most of my professional life was spent as an independent operator. The petroleum industry, especially for the independent operator, is still the most exciting business a man can be in. Exploration, hunting for new supplies of oil and gas, backing your own judgment, is, as ever, the most absorbing part of it. Wildcatting. That's how I started in my early twenties. I look forward immensely to going back to that, and becoming a wildcatter again."

How will he begin his new wildcatting career?

"I shall start by looking for some leasing and drilling opportunities, starting in the Permian Basin, which covers New Mexico and West Texas, from there, possibly, going into the Rockies. The Gulf area is pretty well picked over. Later, perhaps, I shall go into refining and marketing again, but not in the short term. To begin with, I shall go for the production of crude, selling it to anybody who wants to buy."

So, at the age of seventy Bob has started to do again what he was doing fifty years ago, as a boy out of college. Will he make another fortune? He laughed. "I don't know about that." He went on laughing. "But is it possible?" He laughed again. "Yes, it's possible." He then talked about a man who in the last three years has made a fortune out of a copper mine in Butte, Montana, a mine which nobody wanted and which he therefore bought for a song because, according to the experts, there was no market for copper. "He didn't come from the Harvard Business School," said Bob. "He used to be a truck driver. But he has common sense, is a good manager, and he's using non-union labor, for which he pays less than half of what you have to pay for unionized labor. And his company is small enough for him to control personally, and it is not a public company.

"This is very important. When a company becomes large and goes public it encounters certain constraints. Size is a problem in itself. Growth beyond a certain point can obstruct the very dynamism which produced it. This applies not only to, let us say, ARCO, but to every other large public oil company, and, indeed, to all large public companies. There is a paradox here. People sometimes ask me, 'If growth creates problems, why did you choose to grow?' The answer is, 'We had to grow to survive.' Survival apart, up to a point size brings advantages. Size enables you to reduce cost per unit, for example. Larger and larger organizations are inevitable. The problems of managing them are going to increase. We complain about our governments, what they do, what they fail to do. The government of the United States employs 12 million people. The sheer size of its operations is bound to bring about inefficiencies.

"There is something cyclic about growth. A company grows and because of its growth becomes more and more successful. Then because of its size it ceases to be dynamic, becomes static. It becomes cumbersome and conservative, cautious and conventional in its thinking. It is responsible to its shareholders, it must conform to rules and regulations, it must perform duties within the national economy. It becomes bureaucratic. This in itself creates the opportunity for the new small company to emerge and become competitive. The existence of the dinosaur creates the opportunity for the wildcatter. But in time the wildcatter may become another dinosaur. This is the process by which capitalism renews its skills, energy and profitability, and rejuvenates itself. There is something in the nature of a law about it.

"A company that expands does not necessarily lose its dynamism and become static. Much depends on whether it goes public or not. The need to grow is usually associated with the need to go public, and it is when the company goes public in its pursuit of growth that the trouble begins. If a public company makes a major investment which turns out to be a mistake, or is going to be thought to be a mistake, that is going to be a reflection on the management. The management will naturally try and cover it up, including, probably, spending good money after bad. A private company that makes a mistake can say, 'Too bad,' and the mistake need not be made public. When you run a public company you operate in a goldfish bowl."

Bob Anderson's decision to begin again as an explorer for oil and gas is a manifestation of his faith in the oil industry. "And of my enthusiasm for it. It is the greatest industry in the world, and the most exciting to be in. It is unique. It is the one true international business. The amount of oil being carried across the oceans of the world at any particular moment defies the imagination. Oil is used everywhere. The largest need for money in the world's money markets is for the purchase of oil. It is valuable everywhere. It is a kind of currency. A cargo of oil is the nearest thing to a cargo of money. It can be converted into money at the drop of a hat. It is hard currency. This has been the case for fifty years. It is an exciting business because having information a few minutes ahead of anybody else can make somebody millions. There is luck, much luck, involved in the success in the oil business. But the oil business is also a unique test of judgment, experience, stamina and nerve."

INDEX

ABOUT THE AUTHOR

One of Britain's leading journalists, Kenneth Harris was born in 1919 in Aberaman, South Wales. He attended Oxford and returned there after the war for two years to study History. After a five-month tour of the United States, representing the Oxford Union, he wrote his first book, *Travelling Tongues*. From 1950 to 1953 he was in Washington, D.C., on assignment for *The Observer*; in the following years he was a correspondent for the paper on a variety of topics. Most recently he has specialized in large-scale interviews both for *The Observer* and for British television (some of which were published in book form under the title *Kenneth Harris Talking To*). Mr. Harris, currently a director and associate editor of *The Observer*, lives in London. His other works include *Conversations, About Britain, Attlee,* and a forthcoming book on Margaret Thatcher.